JOHN WILDER

Earth Covered Homes

Contents

1

Introduction

I'm John Wilder, a self-builder and architect, and for most of my career, I've been fascinated by the idea of living off the grid. I've worked on dozens of projects where we aim to reduce the environmental footprint of a home, but it wasn't until recently, while working on an off-grid project in the remote countryside, that I stumbled upon something that completely changed the way I think about sustainable living—earth-covered homes.

Imagine this: You wake up to the sound of birds chirping, and as you look outside, there's no bustling city in sight. Instead, you see rolling green hills, with nature wrapping around your home like a comforting blanket. The air feels different, fresher. The view opens up to a landscape that looks untouched by human hands. But here's the catch—you're *inside* your home.

You might think, "Am I living in a cave?" Or, "Is this a house straight out of a Hobbit movie?" Nope, this is an earth-covered home, and it's designed to blend so seamlessly with the natural world that it feels like it belongs there. These homes are built into or beneath the earth, offering a unique combination of beauty, sustainability, and energy efficiency.

The family living in this home, the one I helped design, is saving a fortune on energy bills. But more than that, they've found a way to live in harmony with the planet. Their home, nestled into the hillside, stays naturally cool in the summer and cozy in the winter, all without the constant hum of an air conditioner or heater. They've reduced their environmental impact, but they've also created a peaceful, beautiful space where they feel truly connected to the land. For me, this project was the turning point—it made me see the potential of earth-covered homes in a whole new light.

I have to say, I was skeptical at first. I'd seen pictures of earth homes and heard people talk about their benefits, but I always thought they looked a little... well, strange. I imagined dark, damp rooms with tiny windows, more like a bunker than a house. But when I stepped inside this home, I was amazed. Natural light poured in through large windows and skylights, the air was fresh, and every room had a warmth to it that I hadn't expected. It didn't feel like you were underground at all. Instead, it felt like the outside world was part of the house.

That's when I knew—this wasn't just a novelty. This was the future of sustainable living. And it got me thinking: Why aren't more people doing this? Why aren't we all building homes that use the earth's natural insulation and stability to our advantage?

So, what makes these homes so special? Let me break it down. First off, they're incredibly energy-efficient. The earth acts as a natural insulator, keeping the inside temperature stable year-round. That means in the summer, the home stays cool without cranking up the air conditioning, and in the winter, it stays warm with minimal heating. This family's energy bills are a fraction of what they used to be when they lived in a traditional house. Plus, they're not just saving money—they're also reducing their carbon footprint, which was a huge goal for them.

But the benefits go beyond energy savings. Earth-covered homes are also incredibly resilient. The thick layer of earth surrounding the home protects it from extreme weather conditions. High winds, heavy rains, even wildfires—none of these are a major threat to a well-designed earth-covered home. And let's not forget about noise. Living in one of these homes is quiet. You don't hear the hustle and bustle of the outside world; instead, you're surrounded by the sounds of nature. It's peaceful in a way that most of us aren't used to in our daily lives.

Now, I know what you might be thinking: "This sounds great, but doesn't living underground mean you're living in the dark?" That was one of my concerns, too. But modern earth-covered homes are designed to bring in plenty of natural light. Skylights, sun tunnels, and large south-facing windows are just a few ways we make sure these homes feel bright and airy. In fact, some rooms in the home I worked on had more natural light than the average city apartment.

As an architect, one of the most exciting things about earth-covered homes is how they let you be creative with the design. You're not limited to traditional shapes or layouts. Want a home with curved walls that follow the contours of a hill? No problem. Want a green roof covered in wildflowers? Easy. These homes don't just blend into the landscape; they enhance it. The home I built with this family almost disappears into the hillside. From a distance, all you can see are the windows peeking out, but up close, you realize it's a spacious, modern house, filled with light and comfort.

For the family, building an earth-covered home wasn't just about energy savings or reducing their environmental impact — though those were big reasons. It was about creating a home that felt like part of the landscape. They wanted a house that didn't feel like it was fighting against the natural world but one that worked with it. And that's exactly what they got.

Working on this project has changed the way I approach building. It's made me rethink the possibilities of home design and construction. Earth-covered homes are more than just a sustainable option; they offer a completely different way of living. They invite you to slow down, connect with nature, and live in a way that feels both practical and beautiful.

As I continue my journey in sustainable building, I'm excited to see where this path leads. I know I'll be designing more earth-covered homes, and I'm eager to share this discovery with others who, like me, are looking for ways to live a little lighter on the earth.

And who knows? Maybe the next time you wake up to the sound of birds chirping, it'll be from inside your own earth-covered home.

What Exactly is an Earth-Covered Home?

At its core, an earth-covered home is a structure that is built into or covered by the natural ground. You may hear other terms like *earth-sheltered* or *earth-bermed* homes, but they all share a similar idea: using the earth as part of the structure. There are different types, each with its own unique design:

1. **Earth-Sheltered Homes** are built mostly underground, with only one or two walls exposed to the outside air. These homes may look like they're tucked into the side of a hill or mound, with their roofs often covered by grass or vegetation.
2. **Earth-Bermed Homes** are partially built into the ground, with earth piled up against the exterior walls, providing natural insulation.
3. **Underground Homes** are, as the name suggests, entirely below ground, with only entryways and perhaps skylights connecting them to the outside world.

While the concept of building homes with the earth as protection might sound unusual, it's actually rooted in ancient history. People have been constructing homes like this for thousands of years, from desert dwellings in the Middle East to hillside homes in Europe. What's exciting is that this ancient concept is making a comeback in a modern, eco-conscious world.

Why People are Choosing Earth-Covered Homes

The reasons for the growing interest in earth-covered homes come down to a few big ideas that are hard to ignore:

1. **Energy Efficiency:** One of the biggest selling points is how energy-efficient these homes are. The earth acts as a natural insulator, keeping homes cool in the summer and warm in the winter. This means less need for heating and cooling systems, which translates into lower energy bills and a smaller carbon footprint. A house that helps the environment *and* saves you money? It's a win-win.

2. **Sustainability:** Earth-covered homes use fewer construction materials compared to traditional homes. Plus, they disturb the natural environment less and can even help preserve local ecosystems. Many homeowners choose to build these homes with recycled or eco-friendly materials, making them even more environmentally friendly.

3. **Aesthetic Appeal:** There's something undeniably beautiful about a home that blends into the landscape. Whether it's a house covered in wildflowers or one tucked into a hillside with large, sunlit windows, these homes feel like they belong to the earth rather than competing with it. For those who value nature and peaceful living, earth-covered homes offer a unique, calming atmosphere.

4. **Durability:** Earth-covered homes are designed to withstand extreme weather conditions better than traditional homes. The thick layers of earth provide natural protection against strong winds, heavy rains, and even fires. In fact, in some regions, these homes are popular choices for people living in areas prone to natural disasters because they are so resilient.

Dispelling the Myths

Even though earth-covered homes have many benefits, some people are hesitant about the idea. Let's tackle a few common myths:

- **Myth 1: Earth-Covered Homes are Dark and Gloomy**
- Many people picture earth-covered homes as dim and cave-like, but that's far from the truth. Modern earth-covered homes are designed with large windows, skylights, and light wells, ensuring that they're bright and filled with natural light. Some homes even have central courtyards that act as light sources for the entire house.

- **Myth 2: They're Damp and Uncomfortable**
- Another misconception is that these homes are prone to dampness or mold because they're underground. While it's true that moisture management is important, today's construction methods use advanced waterproofing techniques and proper ventilation systems to keep the interior dry and comfortable. In fact, many earth-covered homes maintain a stable indoor temperature year-round, reducing the need for heating or air conditioning.

- **Myth 3: They're Expensive and Difficult to Build**
- Earth-covered homes can sometimes cost more upfront than traditional homes, mainly due to excavation and waterproofing needs. However, over time, they can save

homeowners money through energy savings and reduced maintenance costs. Plus, with the growing interest in sustainable living, there are more architects and builders specializing in earth-covered designs, making the process easier than it used to be.

A Real-Life Example: The Stevens Family's Earth-Covered Home

To really bring this to life, let's look at a real-world example. The Stevens family wanted to lower their carbon footprint and live a more sustainable life. They were also drawn to the idea of a home that blended with nature. After months of planning, they built an earth-sheltered home in the countryside, with their roof covered in local wildflowers and large windows facing south to capture the sun's heat in the winter.

The result? Not only did they reduce their energy bills by 50%, but they also created a peaceful, beautiful space that made them feel connected to the earth. Their kids love playing on the grassy roof, and they've even started growing vegetables in their own garden on top of the home. As the seasons change, their home stays cool in the summer and warm in the winter, without needing to crank up the air conditioning or heater.

Conclusion: Embracing a New Way to Live

Earth-covered homes offer a unique way of living that is both practical and beautiful. They bring together sustainability, energy efficiency, and aesthetics in a way that's hard to beat. Whether you're driven by the desire to reduce your environmental impact, save on energy bills, or simply live in a home that feels more connected to nature, earth-covered homes provide a fresh, exciting option.

As we continue to rethink the way we live, build, and consume, homes that work with the earth instead of against it might just be the future. And who knows? Maybe your next home could be beneath the surface, tucked away in the landscape, offering both shelter and serenity.

Now that we've explored what an earth-covered home is and why they're so appealing, let's dive into one of their biggest advantages—how they help the environment and reduce your carbon footprint.

2

What is an Earth-Covered Home?

Did you know that homes built into the earth are naturally insulated, reducing energy needs by a whopping 60%? That's right. While it may seem like a new concept, this ancient building method is making a strong comeback—and for good reason. Earth-covered homes combine sustainability, comfort, and beauty in a way that most traditional homes can't. But what exactly are they, and why are they so effective at keeping energy use so low? Let's dig in.

Defining Earth-Covered Homes

To understand earth-covered homes, we first need to break down the different types, because they come in several varieties—each with its own unique approach to using the earth as a building material.

Earth-Sheltered Homes

These are homes where the earth covers most of the structure. Typically, an earth-sheltered home is either built into the side of a hill or partially underground, with only one or two walls exposed to the outside air. Imagine a cozy home with one side open to the sun and the rest nestled into a hillside. The earth around the home acts like a natural blanket, insulating it from temperature extremes. This is what makes earth-sheltered homes so energy-efficient. They stay cool in the summer and warm in the winter with minimal heating and cooling needs.

Earth-Bermed Homes

An earth-bermed home is similar to an earth-sheltered one, but instead of being partially or fully underground, it's a house with earth piled up against its exterior walls. This type of home often looks more like a traditional house, but with earth mounded around the sides to provide insulation. Think of it as giving your home a protective jacket made of soil! Earth-bermed homes take advantage of the insulating properties of the ground without fully immersing the house beneath the surface.

Underground Homes

Lastly, we have underground homes. These are, as the name suggests, built entirely beneath the surface of the earth. The only visible parts are typically the entryways or skylights. These homes are often designed to use natural light, with courtyards or cleverly placed windows to bring in sunshine.

While it may seem like they'd be dark or cold, underground homes are often incredibly comfortable, thanks to that natural insulation and smart design.

Now that we've defined the types, you might be wondering why we'd ever consider living under or surrounded by earth. Well, this isn't just a modern fad—humans have been using the earth as a protective and insulating material for thousands of years.

Historical Roots: Living with the Earth

While the idea of earth-covered homes feels innovative, it's actually rooted in ancient traditions. People have been living in structures built into the earth for millennia. Take cave dwellings, for instance. In regions like Cappadocia in Turkey or Matera in Italy, people carved homes directly into the earth. These ancient structures provided natural insulation and protection from the elements.

In the Middle Ages, some homes were partially dug into the ground to create natural temperature control, which was especially useful in harsh climates. In arid regions, underground dwellings protected people from the extreme heat during the day and the cold at night. These homes offered a sustainable, practical solution long before modern heating and cooling systems were even an option.

Fast forward to the 20th century, when architects like Frank Lloyd Wright began advocating for designs that blended more harmoniously with the environment. His famous "Fallingwater" house wasn't earth-covered, but it marked the beginning of a movement to integrate natural landscapes into home design. Earth-covered homes have since found their way into this trend, evolving from ancient practicality into a modern choice for eco-conscious homeowners.

Modern Resurgence: The Rise of Sustainable Architecture

Today, earth-covered homes are seeing a resurgence, driven by a growing interest in sustainability and reducing energy consumption. As we become more aware of our environmental impact, these homes offer a way to live more lightly on the planet. They are part of a broader movement in sustainable architecture—homes that work with nature, not against it.

Modern earth-covered homes are much more sophisticated than their ancient counterparts. We now have advanced materials for waterproofing, better ways to bring in natural light, and innovative design techniques that make these homes not only practical but also beautiful. You'll find homes with green roofs covered in plants, sun-filled interiors, and outdoor spaces that feel more like extensions of the landscape than separate structures.

But it's not just about the environment. These homes also offer something that traditional houses often don't: a deep sense of peace and connection to the earth. The earth around you acts as both a sound barrier and a temperature regulator, creating a space that's quiet, calm, and comfortable year-round. It's no wonder more people are drawn to this type of living.

Why It's Different from Traditional Homes

So, how are earth-covered homes different from traditional homes? For starters, they use the earth itself as part of their structure, which makes them fundamentally more energy-efficient. In a traditional home, insulation materials are added to the walls and roof to keep the temperature inside stable. But in an earth-covered home, the surrounding soil acts as natural insulation, making heating and cooling systems far less necessary.

Another key difference is their ability to blend into the natural landscape. Unlike traditional homes, which often stand out against their surroundings, earth-covered homes are designed to harmonize with the environment. They can disappear into a hillside, look like part of a forest floor, or feature green roofs that create a living, breathing canopy of plants. This natural integration makes them less intrusive to the landscape and more sustainable overall.

Lastly, earth-covered homes tend to be more resilient. The thick layer of earth surrounding the home protects it from harsh weather, such as high winds, heavy rains, and even fires.

These homes are built to last, offering not just sustainability but long-term durability.

A Unique Earth-Sheltered Home: The Smiths' Journey

To give you a real-world example, let me tell you about the Smith family. They decided to build an earth-sheltered home on a piece of land overlooking a small valley. Their vision was to create a space that blended into the hillside and minimized their environmental impact. They worked with architects who specialized in sustainable design, and together, they created a home that not only met their energy-efficiency goals but also became a sanctuary for the whole family.

The Smiths' home is partially buried in the hillside, with just one side open to the valley. The roof is covered in native grasses and wildflowers, and large south-facing windows bring in natural light, helping to heat the home during the winter months. Their energy bills dropped by 70%, and they've enjoyed the peace and quiet that comes from living in a home that feels like part of the landscape. What's more, their home is a conversation starter—friends and neighbors are fascinated by its design and are often surprised by how modern and spacious it feels inside.

Conclusion:

Earth-covered homes are a remarkable blend of ancient wisdom and modern sustainability. They provide energy efficiency, beauty, and resilience, all while allowing us to live in harmony with the planet. As we move towards a more eco-conscious future, these homes offer a glimpse into what sustainable living can look like—where nature and architecture meet to create spaces that are both practical and inspiring.

Now that we understand what earth-covered homes are, let's explore their eco-friendly benefits and how they can help us reduce our carbon footprint.

Why Choose Earth-Covered Homes?

You might be wondering, with all the types of homes available, why someone would choose an earth-covered home. The answer lies in the unique combination of benefits these homes offer. They're not just about sustainability; they're about living in a way that feels good for both the planet and the people who live there. Let's break down the key reasons why more and more homeowners are choosing to live beneath the surface.

Environmental Benefits and a Lower Carbon Footprint

One of the biggest reasons people are drawn to earth-covered homes is the environmental impact—or rather, the lack of one. These homes are designed to use fewer resources, both in their construction and during day-to-day living. Because they use the earth as a natural insulator, earth-covered homes drastically reduce the amount of energy needed to keep the interior comfortable.

Heating and cooling are two of the biggest energy consumers in any home, but in an earth-covered home, the temperature is regulated naturally by the surrounding soil. This means less reliance on air conditioning in the summer and heating in the winter. Many homeowners report a reduction in energy consumption of up to 60% compared to traditional homes. That's a huge saving—not just for your wallet, but for the planet, too. When you reduce your energy usage, you also reduce your carbon footprint. Living in an earth-covered home means fewer greenhouse gas emissions, helping to combat climate change.

In addition to energy savings, these homes often use sustainable building materials, like recycled concrete or locally sourced timber, reducing the environmental cost of construction. Some homes even incorporate green roofs, where vegetation grows on top, absorbing rainwater, providing insulation, and creating habitats for wildlife.

Long-Term Financial Savings Through Energy Efficiency

Now, let's talk about the financial benefits—because while helping the environment is great, saving money is something we can all get behind. Earth-covered homes aren't just eco-friendly; they're also budget-friendly in the long run. The natural insulation provided by the earth significantly reduces energy costs, which means lower utility bills month after month.

At first glance, building an earth-covered home might seem more expensive than a conventional home, mainly due to excavation and special design considerations. But here's the thing: once it's built, an earth-covered home is incredibly low-maintenance. With less need for heating, cooling, and exterior upkeep (no re-roofing or repainting), the ongoing costs of maintaining an earth-covered home are much lower. Over time, those initial construction costs are quickly offset by the savings in energy and maintenance.

Imagine not having to worry about your home's roof blowing off during a storm, or seeing your heating bill spike during the winter. That peace of mind, combined with consistent long-term savings, makes earth-covered homes a smart investment for the future.

Aesthetic Appeal and Blending with Natural Landscapes

One of the most striking things about earth-covered homes is how they look. These homes don't sit on top of the land; they become part of it. Whether built into a hillside, covered in a grassy berm, or designed with a green roof that bursts into bloom each spring, earth-covered homes have a unique aesthetic that's hard to match.

For many people, this natural design is more than just about looks—it's about creating a space that feels connected to the earth. Instead of clearing land and leveling hills to build a traditional home, earth-covered homes work with the landscape. They blend into their surroundings in a way that feels harmonious and peaceful.

These homes can look as modern or as rustic as you want, but no matter the style, there's something calming about living in a home that feels like it's part of the natural world. Large windows can open up to stunning views, and green roofs can turn your home into a living part of the ecosystem. For those who want a home that offers beauty and serenity, earth-covered homes provide a design that enhances the landscape rather than competing with it.

Health Benefits from Stable Indoor Temperatures

Believe it or not, earth-covered homes can also offer health benefits. One of the most important is the stable indoor temperature that these homes provide. Because the earth acts as a natural insulator, temperatures inside an earth-covered home remain fairly consistent throughout the year. You're not dealing with the extremes of hot summer days or freezing winter nights, which means you're less reliant on artificial heating and cooling systems.

This stability doesn't just make the home more comfortable—it can also be better for your health. For one, you won't experience the dryness that often comes with using central heating in the winter. And because these homes are so well-insulated, they tend to be quieter, offering a peaceful, stress-free environment that's perfect for relaxing and unwinding.

Additionally, with the right ventilation systems in place, earth-covered homes can have excellent air quality. These homes are often designed with natural ventilation in mind, which helps to circulate fresh air without the need for artificial systems that can sometimes lead to dry or stale air. For families who are conscious of creating a healthy living space, earth-covered homes offer a safe, comfortable environment.

A Story of Downsizing and Going Eco-Friendly

Let me share a story about a couple I worked with a few years ago, Sarah and James, who decided to downsize and go eco-friendly. They had spent years in a large suburban home that was expensive to maintain and didn't align with their desire to live more sustainably. After their kids moved out, they started exploring more sustainable housing options. That's when they discovered earth-covered homes.

Sarah and James weren't just looking to save money on bills (although that was certainly a factor); they wanted a home that would allow them to live in a way that felt more connected to the environment. After some research, they found a piece of land in a rural area with a natural slope—perfect for an earth-sheltered home.

Working with an architect, they designed a beautiful home that blended into the landscape. With a green roof full of wildflowers and large south-facing windows that filled the house with natural light, their new home was a far cry from the traditional suburban house they had left behind. They didn't just reduce their energy bills by 50%—they found themselves living a simpler, more peaceful life. They started gardening on their roof, grew vegetables in their backyard, and enjoyed the quiet that came with living in a home so well-insulated from the outside world.

For Sarah and James, downsizing to an earth-covered home wasn't just about saving money. It was about aligning their lifestyle with their values—living more sustainably, reducing their environmental impact, and creating a home that felt like a natural extension of the landscape. Their experience is a perfect example of how choosing an earth-covered home can be about much more than just the practical benefits.

Conclusion:

Choosing an earth-covered home offers a combination of environmental, financial, and aesthetic benefits that are hard to beat. These homes allow you to live in harmony with nature, reduce your energy consumption, and create a peaceful, healthy living environment. Whether you're looking to save money, reduce your carbon footprint, or simply live in a home that feels like it's part of the natural world, earth-covered homes offer a unique and compelling option for sustainable living.

Now that we've explored the benefits of earth-covered homes, let's dive into one of their most exciting aspects—how they help you save energy and money in the long run.

Dispelling the Myths

When people first hear about earth-covered homes, they often have a few misconceptions that might make them hesitate. Maybe you've even thought about these yourself: *Aren't earth-covered homes dark, damp, or difficult to live in?* The idea of living in a home that's partially or fully surrounded by earth can feel unfamiliar at first, but I'm here to clear up a few of the biggest myths and show you why these homes are actually an incredibly smart choice.

Myth 1: Earth-Covered Homes are Dark, Damp, and Unlivable

One of the most common misconceptions is that earth-covered homes are dark, musty spaces, more like caves than livable homes. It's easy to see why people might think this—the idea of living surrounded by dirt brings to mind visions of low light, poor ventilation, and dampness. However, modern earth-covered homes are the exact opposite. Thanks to smart design techniques and advanced materials, these homes are bright, airy, and comfortable.

Let's talk about light first. Modern earth-covered homes are built with large, strategically placed windows, often facing south to maximize natural light. Skylights, light wells, and sun tunnels are also used to flood the interior with sunlight, ensuring the home feels open and inviting, not dark or enclosed.

In fact, many earth-covered homes receive as much, if not more, natural light than traditional homes, especially when designed with passive solar principles in mind.

As for dampness, this concern is easily managed with proper waterproofing techniques. Builders use advanced waterproof membranes, drainage systems, and ventilation to keep moisture out. In some cases, earth-covered homes are actually better at maintaining a dry, consistent indoor environment than above-ground homes because the surrounding earth helps regulate humidity. Far from feeling like a damp cave, these homes offer stable, comfortable conditions year-round.

Myth 2: Earth-Covered Homes Aren't as Durable as Traditional Homes

Another myth is that earth-covered homes are less durable than traditional homes, but in reality, they're often much *more* durable. The earth surrounding the structure actually provides a natural shield from extreme weather, acting as a protective layer. In regions prone to high winds, storms, or even wildfires, earth-covered homes are often safer than their conventional counterparts.

Let's compare a traditional home and an earth-covered home in terms of durability. A typical above-ground house is exposed to the elements: wind, rain, sun, snow, and even temperature fluctuations that cause wear and tear over time. Roofs need to be replaced, siding can warp or rot, and the home's exterior is constantly battling the forces of nature. Earth-covered homes, on the other hand, have most of their exterior surfaces shielded by earth, which dramatically reduces exposure to the elements. This means fewer repairs and lower maintenance costs over time.

In areas that experience extreme weather events, like hurricanes or tornadoes, earth-covered homes are particularly resilient. The earth acts as a barrier against high winds, and the lower profile of the home means there's less structure for the wind to grab onto. These homes are also more resistant to fire, since the earth covering them doesn't burn. In short, earth-covered homes offer a level of natural protection that traditional homes can't match.

Myth 3: Living Underground Isn't Safe

Another question people often ask is: *Is it safe to live underground?* This is a valid concern, especially when you think about things like structural integrity, earthquakes, or the possibility of flooding. But here's the good news: modern earth-covered homes are designed with these safety concerns in mind, and they're built to be just as safe—if not safer—than traditional homes.

In terms of structural integrity, these homes are built using reinforced materials like concrete, steel, and specialized waterproof membranes to ensure they are strong and secure. The surrounding earth adds a layer of stability, and when designed properly, earth-covered homes can withstand natural forces better than traditional homes. Earthquake-prone regions, for example, often benefit from the added stability that comes with an underground or earth-bermed structure, as the ground around the home helps absorb shock waves.

Flooding is another concern people have when they think about living underground. However, modern earth-covered homes are designed with advanced drainage systems that channel water away from the home. The construction includes layers of waterproofing to prevent moisture from seeping in, ensuring that the interior stays dry, even in heavy rainfall. In many cases, an earth-covered home can be less prone to water damage than a traditional home, especially when situated on a slope that naturally directs water away from the structure.

Maintenance Concerns: Easier Than You Might Think

Maintenance is a topic that often comes up when discussing earth-covered homes. Some people worry that maintaining an earth-covered home is more complicated than a traditional house, but the truth is, they're often much easier to maintain.

Traditional homes require regular upkeep: roof repairs, siding maintenance, painting, and sealing, to name a few. Earth-covered homes, on the other hand, don't have the same exposure to the elements, so they require less exterior maintenance. Green roofs (if your earth-covered home includes one) might need occasional trimming or planting, but they're far less prone to wear and tear than a conventional roof that needs to be replaced every 20 to 30 years.

With proper construction and waterproofing, the interior of an earth-covered home also requires little more maintenance than a standard home. You won't need to worry about leaks, drafts, or extreme temperature swings because the earth acts as a consistent insulating layer. The main maintenance concern for earth-covered homes is ensuring that drainage systems are working properly, but that's a minor issue compared to the ongoing maintenance costs of traditional homes.

Case Study: The Harris Family's Modern Earth-Covered Home

To give you a real-world example, let's look at the Harris family, who built a modern earth-covered home in a hilly region known for its strong winds and occasional wildfires. When they first decided to build an earth-sheltered home, their friends and neighbors were skeptical, raising concerns about light, dampness, and safety. But the Harris family was determined to live sustainably and wanted a home that blended with the landscape rather than standing out.

Their architect designed a home built into the hillside, with large windows facing the valley to bring in plenty of natural light. The home's roof was covered in native grasses, which not only provided additional insulation but also helped the house blend seamlessly into the surroundings. Inside, the Harris family enjoys consistent, comfortable temperatures without relying on air conditioning in the summer or heavy heating in the winter.

During a particularly bad storm season, when neighboring houses experienced roof damage and power outages, the Harris family's earth-covered home stayed safe and dry. The thick earth covering the house protected them from the high winds, and their energy-efficient design meant they could rely on minimal power usage even when the grid went down.

The Harris family now advocates for earth-covered homes, and their experience has helped dispel many of the myths their friends and neighbors once had. Their home is a testament to how modern earth-covered designs can provide not only beauty and sustainability but also safety and comfort.

Now that you know what an earth-covered home is and have a better understanding of their benefits and safety, let's dive deeper into the environmental benefits that truly set these homes apart from traditional housing.

3

The Eco-Friendly Benefits

ere's a shocking fact: *Construction and buildings account for 40% of global carbon emissions.* Yes, almost half of the carbon footprint comes from the buildings we live and work in. But what if your home could actually help reduce that impact instead of contributing to it? Enter earth-covered homes, a sustainable solution that not only lowers your energy usage but also works in harmony with nature. Let's explore how building into the earth can drastically reduce your carbon footprint and create a home that's as gentle on the planet as it is comfortable for you.

Reducing Your Carbon Footprint

When we talk about living sustainably, reducing our carbon footprint is at the top of the list. Earth-covered homes are particularly effective at this because they use the earth itself as part of the structure, which naturally reduces the need for many of the energy-intensive systems traditional homes rely on. Here's how:

1. Conserving Natural Resources by Building into the Earth

Building an earth-covered home is fundamentally different from constructing a traditional house. Rather than using large amounts of materials like wood, brick, or steel, earth-covered homes are built right into the ground. By using the earth as a primary building component, you're conserving natural resources that would otherwise be used for walls, roofing, and insulation.

The process of building into the earth means less material waste during construction and fewer resources extracted from nature. Instead of relying on energy-intensive manufacturing processes to create insulation, the earth itself provides a natural insulating layer that surrounds the home. This method significantly reduces the overall demand for industrial materials and helps preserve our planet's precious resources.

2. Natural Insulation That Reduces Energy Usage

One of the most impressive features of an earth-covered home is its ability to maintain stable temperatures without much help from modern heating or cooling systems. In a traditional home, insulation is added to walls and ceilings to help regulate indoor temperature, but even the best insulation can only do so much. You still need to rely heavily on air conditioners in the summer and heating systems in the winter, which adds up to a lot of energy consumption—and a hefty carbon footprint.

In contrast, earth-covered homes are naturally insulated by the surrounding soil, which acts as a thermal buffer. The temperature of the earth just a few feet below the surface is remarkably stable throughout the year, staying cooler in the summer and warmer in the winter. This natural insulation means the interior of an earth-covered home stays at a comfortable temperature without the need for constant air conditioning or heating.

Think about it this way: in the heat of summer, while traditional homes are running their AC units on full blast, an earth-covered home stays cool simply because the earth absorbs and dissipates heat. And during the winter, the same principle applies—the earth helps retain warmth, so you don't have to crank up the thermostat. This reduced reliance on energy-hungry HVAC systems translates into lower energy bills and a much smaller carbon footprint.

3. Minimizing the Need for HVAC Systems

Because earth-covered homes are naturally insulated, they require far less energy for heating and cooling. In many cases, homeowners can get by with minimal HVAC systems—or none at all. Some earth-covered homes are designed with passive solar principles, meaning they use the sun's natural heat and light to warm the home in the winter, reducing the need for artificial heating systems.

For example, south-facing windows can allow sunlight to pour in during the colder months, warming the interior naturally. In the summer, when the sun is higher in the sky, strategically placed overhangs or the earth itself can provide shade, keeping the home cool. This thoughtful design eliminates the need for air conditioners or large heating systems, making the home not only energy-efficient but also more environmentally friendly.

The overall energy usage of an earth-covered home can be as much as 80% lower than that of a conventional house. That's a significant reduction in the use of fossil fuels and other nonrenewable energy sources, helping to cut down on greenhouse gas emissions.

4. Less Disruption to Wildlife and Ecosystems

One of the less obvious but equally important benefits of earth-covered homes is their ability to blend into the natural landscape without causing major disruptions to local wildlife and ecosystems. Traditional homes, with their large footprints and cleared land, often disrupt the natural habitats of animals, plants, and other species. Trees are cut down, soil is displaced, and ecosystems are disturbed in the process.

Earth-covered homes, however, are designed to work *with* the land rather than against it. Because they are built into hillsides or covered with vegetation, these homes can preserve much of the natural landscape. Green roofs, for example, provide a habitat for birds, insects, and small animals. The impact on local wildlife is minimal, and in some cases, these homes even enhance biodiversity by creating new habitats on top of and around the structure.

By choosing an earth-covered home, you're not only reducing your own carbon footprint, but you're also helping to protect the ecosystems that surround your property. This harmonious relationship with nature is one of the core values of sustainable living.

A Real-Life Comparison: Earth-Covered vs. Traditional Homes

Let's take a look at how this works in the real world. A few years ago, I had the pleasure of working with two families—one building a traditional home and the other opting for an earth-covered home. Both homes were built in the same region, with similar square footage, but the results couldn't have been more different.

The Smiths, who went with a traditional home, spent the first summer running their air conditioner almost constantly to keep their house cool. Their energy bill for July alone was over $300. When winter came around, they found themselves using more heating than they expected, and their energy costs continued to climb.

The Johnsons, on the other hand, built an earth-covered home on a small hillside. Their home stayed naturally cool throughout the summer, thanks to the surrounding earth. In fact, they didn't need to use air conditioning at all. During the winter, they relied mostly on the sun's natural heat and a small, energy-efficient heating system. By the end of the year, the Johnsons' total energy costs were less than half of what the Smiths had paid—and they felt great knowing they were using far less energy.

The Johnsons' experience isn't unique. Earth-covered homes are designed to take advantage of natural insulation, and the savings are real. Plus, it's not just about the money—they also significantly reduced their carbon footprint, contributing to a more sustainable future for all of us.

Conclusion:

Reducing your carbon footprint doesn't have to mean compromising on comfort or beauty. With earth-covered homes, you get the best of both worlds: a home that conserves natural resources, uses less energy, and blends seamlessly with the environment. By embracing this type of eco-friendly architecture, you can live more sustainably while still enjoying all the comforts of modern living.

Now that we've seen how earth-covered homes help the environment, let's explore the long-term financial benefits of living in one—because being eco-friendly can also mean saving money.

Sustainable Building Materials

One of the most compelling aspects of earth-covered homes is how they embrace sustainability not only in their design but also in the materials used to build them. The materials chosen for an earth-covered home are often as eco-friendly as the structure itself, helping homeowners minimize their environmental impact at every step. Whether it's rammed earth, recycled materials, or natural resources, earth-covered homes are built with sustainability in mind from the ground up—literally.

Let's explore the types of materials commonly used in these homes and how they contribute to a more sustainable way of living.

1. Types of Materials Used in Earth-Covered Homes

When it comes to building an earth-covered home, the materials chosen can make all the difference. In many cases, the key is selecting materials that have a low environmental impact and work in harmony with the earth that surrounds the home. Some of the most common materials include:

- **Rammed Earth:** This is one of the oldest and most sustainable building materials around. Rammed earth involves compressing a mixture of soil, clay, and sometimes a small amount of cement into thick walls. These walls are not only incredibly durable, but they also provide excellent thermal mass, helping to regulate the temperature inside the home. Because the materials are locally sourced, rammed earth construction has a very low carbon footprint.

- **Recycled Materials:** Many earth-covered homes make use of recycled or reclaimed materials. These can include recycled concrete, reclaimed wood, or even materials like recycled steel and glass. Using recycled materials reduces the demand for new resources and helps divert waste from landfills, making it a key part of sustainable building practices.

- **Natural Stone and Wood:** In some earth-covered homes, natural stone is used for structural or decorative purposes. Stone is an abundant resource, and when sourced locally, it can contribute to the overall sustainability of the home. Similarly, responsibly sourced wood is often used for framing or interior finishes, providing warmth and natural beauty.

- **Green Roof Materials:** Many earth-covered homes feature green roofs, which are covered in vegetation. These roofs are not only beautiful but also provide insulation, reduce stormwater runoff, and create habitats for wildlife. The materials used in green roofs, such as lightweight soil mixtures and plant-friendly membranes, are chosen to support sustainability while enhancing the home's energy efficiency.

By using materials that are either naturally abundant or re-cycled, earth-covered homes minimize their environmental impact, both during construction and throughout the life of the building. But there's more to sustainability than just using the right materials—it's also about how those materials are chosen and used.

2. How These Materials Contribute to Sustainability

The materials used in earth-covered homes aren't just eco-friendly because they come from natural or recycled sources. They're sustainable because they work in harmony with the home's design, reducing the need for artificial heating, cooling, and maintenance. Let's look at how these materials contribute to a greener, more sustainable way of living.

- **Thermal Mass and Insulation:** Materials like rammed earth, natural stone, and green roof systems provide excellent thermal mass, which means they absorb heat during the day and release it slowly at night. This helps maintain a stable indoor temperature without the need for excessive energy use. Rammed earth, in particular, has the ability to moderate temperature fluctuations, keeping the home cool in the summer and warm in the winter.
- **Durability and Low Maintenance:** Many of the materials used in earth-covered homes are incredibly durable, which reduces the need for frequent repairs or replacements. Rammed earth and natural stone, for example, can last for centuries with minimal maintenance. This durability means that fewer resources are needed for upkeep over time, contributing to the overall sustainability of the home.
- **Reducing Waste:** Using recycled materials not only reduces the need for new resources but also helps minimize waste. By incorporating materials that would otherwise end up in a landfill, earth-covered homes contribute to a more circular economy. In some cases, construction waste from other projects can be repurposed, giving materials like concrete and steel a second life.
- **Local Sourcing:** Whenever possible, materials for earth-covered homes are sourced locally. This reduces the environmental impact associated with transportation and helps support local economies. Local sourcing also ensures that the materials used are well-suited to the local climate

and geography, further enhancing the sustainability of the home.

Each of these factors plays a part in making earth-covered homes some of the most eco-friendly structures you can build. But there's an even deeper philosophy behind the choice of materials in sustainable construction, known as "cradle-to-cradle."

3. The Cradle-to-Cradle Philosophy in Earth-Covered Construction

The concept of *cradle-to-cradle* design is all about creating systems that are regenerative and waste-free. It's a step beyond traditional recycling, focusing on how materials can be continuously reused or returned to the earth without causing harm. In the context of earth-covered homes, cradle-to-cradle thinking is applied by choosing materials that either biodegrade naturally or can be recycled endlessly.

For example, rammed earth is a perfect fit for the cradle-to-cradle philosophy. At the end of its life, the earthen walls can simply be broken down and returned to the soil, leaving no harmful waste behind. Similarly, materials like natural stone and wood can decompose or be repurposed with minimal environmental impact.

This approach to building ensures that even at the end of a home's life, it won't become a burden on the environment. Instead, the materials can be absorbed back into the earth or reused in new projects, creating a closed-loop system that minimizes waste and maximizes sustainability.

Cradle-to-cradle design also encourages architects and builders to think about the entire life cycle of a home, from construction to demolition (or deconstruction). This long-term thinking is a key component of sustainable architecture, and it's one of the reasons why earth-covered homes are gaining popularity among eco-conscious homeowners.

4. The Benefits of Low Embodied Energy in Materials

One of the most important considerations in sustainable construction is *embodied energy*, which refers to the total amount of energy required to extract, process, transport, and install building materials. The lower the embodied energy of a material, the more sustainable it is. Earth-covered homes excel in this area because many of the materials used—like rammed earth and local stone—have very low embodied energy.

For instance, rammed earth requires minimal processing compared to materials like concrete or steel, which must be manufactured in energy-intensive factories. And because many of the materials are sourced locally, transportation costs (and the associated carbon emissions) are kept to a minimum. This means that from the very beginning, earth-covered homes have a smaller environmental footprint than traditional homes.

By choosing materials with low embodied energy, earth-covered homes not only reduce their carbon footprint during construction but also set the stage for a lifetime of energy savings. It's a win-win for the environment and for homeowners looking to build sustainably.

A Story of Eco-Friendly Construction: GreenEarth Builders

To bring these ideas to life, let me tell you about a construction company called *GreenEarth Builders*, who specialize in using eco-friendly materials for earth-covered homes. Based in the Pacific Northwest, this company has made a name for itself by blending innovative design with sustainable building practices.

One of their most impressive projects was the *Willow House*, an earth-covered home built for a couple who wanted to minimize their carbon footprint while creating a beautiful, comfortable living space. GreenEarth Builders used locally sourced materials, including rammed earth for the walls and natural stone for the foundation. The roof was designed as a green space, planted with native grasses and wildflowers that helped insulate the home while providing a habitat for local wildlife.

What set GreenEarth Builders apart was their commitment to the cradle-to-cradle philosophy. Every material used in the Willow House was chosen with sustainability in mind. From the reclaimed wood used for the interior framing to the recycled steel used for structural supports, every element of the home was designed to be reused or returned to the earth at the end of its life.

The result? A stunning, energy-efficient home that blended seamlessly into the surrounding landscape. The couple who owned the Willow House were thrilled with the outcome—not only did their home exceed their expectations for comfort and beauty, but it also gave them peace of mind knowing they were living in harmony with the planet.

GreenEarth Builders continue to push the boundaries of sustainable construction, proving that it's possible to build homes that are as eco-friendly as they are beautiful. Their work is a shining example of how the right materials, combined with thoughtful design, can create homes that stand the test of time—without sacrificing the health of the environment.

Conclusion: The materials used in earth-covered homes are more than just building blocks—they are a crucial part of the home's sustainability. By choosing materials with low embodied energy, embracing the cradle-to-cradle philosophy, and working in harmony with nature, earth-covered homes offer a path toward a greener future. These homes don't just reduce their environmental impact during construction; they continue to benefit the planet throughout their entire lifecycle.

Now that we've explored the materials used in earth-covered homes, let's turn our attention to how these homes manage water and land, preserving ecosystems and supporting sustainable living.

Water and Land Management

Earth-covered homes don't just sit on the land—they actively work with it. A key part of their environmental benefits comes from how they manage water and use land efficiently. In this section, we'll explore how these homes help manage stormwater, reduce the urban heat island effect, and integrate sustainable land-use practices like permaculture. When you build an earth-covered home, you're not just creating a structure—you're making a positive impact on the surrounding environment.

1. Managing Stormwater with Berms and Earth

One of the most important features of earth-covered homes is their ability to manage water naturally, especially stormwater. In traditional homes, stormwater often runs off roofs and paved surfaces, flowing into storm drains and, in some cases, overwhelming local water systems. This runoff can carry pollutants, contribute to flooding, and disrupt local ecosystems. Earth-covered homes, by contrast, are designed to absorb and manage rainwater more effectively, reducing the strain on municipal water systems and minimizing environmental damage.

The key to this lies in the way earth-covered homes are built. Many of these homes use **berms**—raised mounds of earth around the structure—to help channel water away from the home and into the surrounding landscape. These berms, along with the earth covering the home, slow down the flow of water, allowing it to be absorbed naturally into the ground. This reduces the risk of flooding and helps recharge local groundwater supplies.

Berms aren't just practical—they can also be beautiful. Many homeowners choose to plant native grasses, wildflowers, or even small shrubs on their berms, turning them into lush, green spaces that contribute to the overall aesthetic of the home. The plants on these berms also play a role in water management, as their root systems help absorb and filter rainwater, preventing erosion and reducing runoff.

In areas prone to heavy rainfall, earth-covered homes offer a sustainable solution to stormwater management. By using the earth itself to control and absorb water, these homes reduce the need for artificial drainage systems and minimize the impact on the environment.

2. Reducing the Urban Heat Island Effect with Green Roofs and Earth Insulation

Urban areas are known for what's called the **urban heat island effect**, a phenomenon where cities tend to be significantly warmer than their rural surroundings. This happens because traditional buildings, roads, and pavements absorb and retain heat during the day and release it slowly at night. The result is higher temperatures, increased energy use for cooling, and a generally less comfortable living environment.

Earth-covered homes, with their natural insulation and **green**

roofs, offer an effective way to combat the urban heat island effect. Green roofs, which are roofs covered in vegetation, help cool the air by providing shade and reducing the amount of heat absorbed by the building. The plants on green roofs also release moisture through a process called evapotranspiration, which cools the surrounding air and creates a more pleasant microclimate.

The earth itself acts as a powerful insulator, preventing heat from entering the home during the day and keeping it cool at night. This reduces the need for air conditioning and lowers energy consumption, which in turn helps decrease the overall temperature in urban areas. In cities where heat waves are becoming more common, earth-covered homes can play a significant role in reducing energy demand and improving comfort.

By integrating earth insulation and green roofs into urban design, we can create cooler, more sustainable cities that are better equipped to handle the effects of climate change. Earth-covered homes provide a model for how we can rethink urban architecture to work *with* the environment, rather than against it.

3. Efficient Use of Land in Urban Environments

As cities grow and space becomes more limited, the efficient use of land is becoming increasingly important. Earth-covered homes offer a creative solution to this challenge. Because they can be built into hillsides or even beneath the surface, they take up less *visible* space than traditional homes, freeing up land for other uses.

In densely populated urban environments, earth-covered homes can be designed to fit seamlessly into the landscape, allowing for more green space on the surface. This means that instead of a neighborhood full of buildings and concrete, you could have a community where homes are hidden beneath parks, gardens, or even playgrounds. The space that would otherwise be occupied by rooftops and walls can be transformed into natural landscapes that provide recreational areas, habitats for wildlife, and more room for vegetation.

In addition to saving space, earth-covered homes can also help reduce the impact of urban sprawl. Instead of expanding cities outward into rural areas, these homes can be integrated into the existing urban fabric, using land more efficiently and reducing the need for further development. This not only preserves natural habitats but also helps create more walkable, livable cities where green space is abundant and easily accessible.

4. How Earth-Covered Homes Can Integrate Permaculture Principles

One of the most exciting possibilities for earth-covered homes is their potential to integrate **permaculture principles** into their design. Permaculture is a system of agriculture and land management that works with nature to create sustainable ecosystems. It's based on principles like using renewable resources, minimizing waste, and creating self-sustaining systems that support both people and the environment.

Earth-covered homes are a natural fit for permaculture because they already embrace many of these principles. By using the earth as insulation, managing water naturally, and blending into the landscape, these homes create a more sustainable way of living. But the benefits don't stop there—earth-covered homes can also be designed to incorporate gardens, food forests, and other permaculture elements that further enhance their environmental impact.

For example, an earth-covered home could be surrounded by a **permaculture garden**, where fruit trees, vegetables, and herbs grow in harmony with the natural environment. These gardens are designed to be self-sustaining, with plants that support each other and create a healthy, biodiverse ecosystem. The home itself becomes part of this system, with rainwater collected from the green roof used to irrigate the garden, and compost from the household supporting the growth of plants.

Permaculture is all about creating systems that are regenerative and sustainable, and earth-covered homes provide the perfect foundation for this kind of living. By integrating permaculture principles, homeowners can create a lifestyle that not only reduces their environmental impact but also supports a thriving ecosystem around their home.

Example: A Community of Earth-Covered Homes with Shared Permaculture Gardens

One community that has embraced this concept is **GreenGrove Village**, a neighborhood of earth-covered homes built with sustainability in mind. Located on the outskirts of a major city, GreenGrove was designed to combine the benefits of earth-covered homes with the principles of permaculture to create a model for eco-friendly urban living.

The homes in GreenGrove are built into the landscape, with green roofs and berms that help manage stormwater and reduce the urban heat island effect. But what really sets this community apart is its shared permaculture garden, which is at the heart of the neighborhood. The garden is a lush, diverse space filled with fruit trees, vegetable patches, herb gardens, and even a small pond that attracts local wildlife.

Each family in the community contributes to the care and upkeep of the garden, and in return, they share in the harvest. The permaculture garden provides fresh, organic produce for the entire community, reducing their reliance on supermarkets and lowering their overall carbon footprint. The design of the homes and garden encourages a deep connection to nature, with residents working together to maintain a self-sustaining system that benefits both people and the environment.

The success of GreenGrove Village has inspired other communities to adopt similar models, showing that earth-covered homes, combined with permaculture, can create sustainable, resilient neighborhoods that are well-suited to the challenges of modern urban living.

Conclusion: Water and land management are critical components of sustainable living, and earth-covered homes excel in both areas. From managing stormwater with berms to reducing the urban heat island effect with green roofs, these homes offer practical, eco-friendly solutions to the challenges of urban development. And by integrating permaculture principles, earth-covered homes can create thriving ecosystems that benefit both the environment and the people who live in them.

Now that we've explored the environmental side of earth-covered homes, it's time to dive into one of their most appealing aspects—how they provide long-term financial and energy benefits. Let's see how living beneath the surface can save you money in the long run.

4

Energy Efficiency and Cost Savings

What if your home could reduce your energy bill by 80%? It might sound too good to be true, but for people living in earth-covered homes, that's often a reality. These homes, built into the earth and using nature's natural insulating properties, are not only environmentally friendly—they can also save you a lot of money. Let's explore how these unique homes take advantage of natural insulation, regulate temperatures, and cut down energy costs while providing a comfortable living environment year-round.

Natural Insulation and Temperature Regulation

One of the key features that sets earth-covered homes apart from traditional homes is their incredible energy efficiency, thanks to natural insulation provided by the earth itself. Traditional homes rely heavily on artificial insulation, heating, and cooling systems to maintain comfortable indoor temperatures. But earth-covered homes use the very ground they're built into as a powerful insulating barrier, creating a more consistent and comfortable living environment while significantly reducing energy usage.

1. How Earth Naturally Provides Superior Insulation

The concept behind natural insulation is simple: the earth has remarkable thermal properties. Just a few feet below the surface, the temperature remains relatively constant throughout the year, regardless of the season. In colder climates, the earth's insulation helps keep homes warmer in the winter, while in hot climates, it prevents overheating in the summer.

For earth-covered homes, the surrounding soil acts as a thick, natural insulating layer that keeps indoor temperatures stable. Think of it as Mother Nature's way of wrapping your home in a cozy, protective blanket. Instead of relying on synthetic materials like fiberglass or foam to insulate the walls, the earth itself does the job. The result? A home that stays cooler in the summer and warmer in the winter, all without the need for excessive energy use.

2. Thermal Mass and Maintaining Constant Indoor Temperatures

Beyond just insulation, earth-covered homes take advantage of something called **thermal mass**. Thermal mass refers to a material's ability to absorb, store, and slowly release heat. The walls of earth-covered homes, often made from materials like rammed earth or concrete, have a high thermal mass, meaning they can absorb heat during the day and release it gradually at night.

Here's how it works: during a hot summer day, the walls of an earth-covered home absorb heat, preventing it from entering the living space. At night, when temperatures drop, the heat stored in the walls is slowly released, keeping the interior warm. This process naturally regulates the temperature inside the home, reducing the need for air conditioning in the summer and heating in the winter.

In colder months, the thermal mass of the walls can store heat from the sun or from a low-energy heating system and release it throughout the night, helping to maintain a comfortable indoor temperature without having to constantly adjust the thermostat. This natural process allows the home to maintain a steady, comfortable temperature with minimal energy use, which translates to significant savings on utility bills.

3. Reducing the Need for Heating and Cooling Systems

The natural insulation and thermal mass of earth-covered homes greatly reduce the need for artificial heating and cooling systems. In a traditional home, the HVAC system is often running constantly—cooling the house in the summer and heating it in the winter. This can lead to high energy consumption, especially in regions with extreme temperatures.

But in an earth-covered home, the temperature remains much more stable. The home's design takes advantage of the earth's insulating properties, keeping the interior cool in the summer and warm in the winter without relying heavily on air conditioning or heating. In some cases, earth-covered homes can eliminate the need for traditional HVAC systems altogether, using only a small supplemental heating or cooling system to maintain comfort.

Take, for example, the use of **passive solar design** in earth-covered homes. Passive solar design involves positioning the home to maximize natural sunlight during the winter and minimize heat gain during the summer. South-facing windows allow sunlight to warm the home during the day, and the thick, insulating walls store that heat, releasing it at night. In the summer, overhangs or berms help shade the windows, preventing excessive heat from entering the home. This simple, yet effective design strategy can further reduce the need for artificial heating and cooling, making the home even more energy-efficient.

A Story of Energy Efficiency: The Colson Family's Cold-Region Earth-Covered Home

To see just how effective natural insulation and thermal mass can be, let's look at the Colson family, who built an earth-covered home in a region known for its harsh winters. The Colsons lived in a traditional home for years, and every winter, their heating bills were sky-high. The cold air would seep through their walls, and despite their best efforts to insulate, their home was always chilly, and their heating system was constantly running.

After learning about earth-covered homes, the Colsons decided to build one into the side of a hill on their property. The natural insulation provided by the earth, combined with the thick rammed earth walls, made a huge difference in their energy use. The first winter in their new home, they noticed something remarkable: their home stayed warm and cozy without their heating system running constantly. They installed a small, energy-efficient heater for particularly cold nights, but most of the time, the home maintained a comfortable temperature on its own.

At the end of the winter, the Colsons compared their energy bills to their old home's. The result? Their heating costs were 75% lower than the previous year. By using the earth as insulation and taking advantage of thermal mass, they were able to reduce their energy consumption drastically—and they were more comfortable than ever before.

Their story highlights the incredible energy-saving potential of earth-covered homes, especially in cold climates. By working with nature instead of against it, the Colsons created a home that not only saved them money but also reduced their environmental impact.

4. Example of Passive Solar Design in Earth-Covered Homes

One of the most effective ways to enhance the natural energy efficiency of an earth-covered home is by incorporating **passive solar design**. This design strategy focuses on using the sun's energy to heat and light the home naturally, without the need for mechanical systems.

In an earth-covered home, passive solar design often begins with the orientation of the building. By positioning the home so that its largest windows face south, the home can capture the sun's warmth during the winter months, when the sun is lower in the sky. The heat from the sun warms the interior during the day, and the thick walls of the home store that heat, slowly releasing it during the night to maintain a comfortable temperature.

During the summer, when the sun is higher in the sky, carefully designed overhangs or berms can shade the windows, preventing too much heat from entering the home. This keeps the interior cool and reduces the need for air conditioning. Combined with the earth's natural insulation, passive solar design allows earth-covered homes to maintain a stable indoor temperature year-round with minimal energy use.

A well-designed earth-covered home with passive solar features can reduce heating and cooling costs by up to 80%, making it not only environmentally friendly but also incredibly cost-effective in the long run.

Conclusion: Earth-covered homes are masters of energy efficiency, thanks to the natural insulating properties of the earth, the thermal mass of their walls, and the use of passive solar design. By working with nature instead of against it, these homes can significantly reduce energy consumption, cutting heating and cooling costs by as much as 80%. The Colson family's experience in their cold-region home shows just how powerful these design features can be, providing comfort and warmth with minimal energy use.

Now that we've explored how earth-covered homes save energy through natural insulation, let's take a closer look at how they can integrate renewable energy sources to create truly sustainable living environments.

Renewable Energy Integration

Building an energy-efficient home doesn't stop with natural insulation and passive design. For many homeowners, the next logical step is incorporating renewable energy systems to create a home that's not only energy-efficient but also self-sustaining. Earth-covered homes are a perfect match for renewable energy solutions like solar, wind, geothermal, and water conservation systems. Together, these technologies can take the sustainability of an earth-covered home to the next level and even allow homeowners to go completely off the grid.

Let's dive into how renewable energy can be integrated into earth-covered homes to create a truly eco-friendly and self-sufficient living environment.

1. Using Solar Panels and Wind Energy with Earth-Covered Homes

Earth-covered homes, with their natural insulation and energy-efficient design, require less power to heat and cool compared to traditional homes. This makes them ideal candidates for pairing with renewable energy sources like **solar panels** and **wind turbines**.

Solar panels are often the first renewable energy solution homeowners consider, and they work exceptionally well with earth-covered homes. While the homes themselves are integrated into the ground, the roof areas, or exposed sections, can be fitted with solar panels to capture the sun's energy. In many designs, the roofs of earth-covered homes are sloped or positioned to maximize sunlight, making them perfect for harnessing solar power.

Solar energy can be used to power the home's electrical systems, and in combination with the natural energy savings from the earth's insulation, many earth-covered homes can generate enough solar power to cover their entire energy needs. Any excess energy can be stored in batteries for use during the night or on cloudy days, ensuring a steady supply of renewable electricity.

Wind energy is another option that can complement solar power, especially in regions where wind is a reliable resource. A small wind turbine installed near the home can generate additional electricity, particularly during winter months when solar energy might be less abundant. By using both solar and wind power, earth-covered homes can create a balanced renewable energy system that provides power throughout the year, regardless of weather conditions.

2. Geothermal Systems for Heating and Cooling

One of the most effective ways to heat and cool an earth-covered home using renewable energy is through **geothermal systems**. Geothermal heating and cooling takes advantage of the stable temperatures just below the earth's surface—an idea that aligns perfectly with the natural insulation properties of earth-covered homes.

Here's how it works: A geothermal system uses a series of underground pipes, known as a **ground-source heat pump**, to exchange heat with the earth. In the winter, the system pulls heat from the ground and distributes it throughout the home. In the summer, it does the opposite, transferring heat from the home back into the cooler earth. Because the temperature below ground remains relatively constant, geothermal systems are incredibly efficient, providing heating and cooling at a fraction of the energy cost of traditional systems.

For earth-covered homes, which are already benefiting from the earth's natural insulation, a geothermal system can further reduce the need for energy-intensive HVAC systems. This creates an incredibly energy-efficient heating and cooling solution that works in harmony with the home's design. Plus, geothermal systems are powered by electricity, which means they can be paired with solar panels or wind turbines to create a completely renewable energy loop for the home.

3. Rainwater Harvesting and Greywater Systems for Self-Sufficiency

Water conservation is another key element of sustainable living, and many earth-covered homes integrate **rainwater harvesting** and **greywater systems** to reduce water usage and increase self-sufficiency.

Rainwater harvesting involves collecting rainwater from the roof or other surfaces and storing it in tanks or cisterns for later use. Earth-covered homes, especially those with green roofs, are ideal for rainwater harvesting because their roofs naturally absorb and channel rainwater. This harvested water can be used for a variety of purposes, such as watering gardens, flushing toilets, or even filtering for drinking water.

Greywater systems take sustainability one step further by recycling water from household activities like washing dishes, laundry, or bathing. This water, which would otherwise go down the drain, can be treated and reused for non-potable purposes, such as irrigation or toilet flushing. By recycling greywater, earth-covered homes reduce the amount of fresh water they need, making them even more environmentally friendly.

When combined, rainwater harvesting and greywater systems allow earth-covered homes to dramatically reduce their reliance on municipal water supplies. In some cases, these homes can become fully self-sufficient in terms of water use, relying entirely on harvested and recycled water for daily needs. This not only conserves water but also reduces the home's overall environmental footprint.

4. How Earth Homes Pair with Off-Grid Systems

For homeowners who want to take sustainability to the next level, going **off-grid** is an exciting possibility. Earth-covered homes are particularly well-suited for off-grid living because they are designed to be energy-efficient and environmentally responsible from the start. By combining renewable energy sources like solar and wind power, geothermal heating and cooling, and water conservation systems, earth-covered homes can operate independently of public utilities.

Off-grid systems typically include solar panels or wind turbines for electricity, batteries for energy storage, a backup generator for emergencies, and systems for water collection and treatment. Because earth-covered homes use far less energy than traditional homes, they require smaller renewable energy systems to meet their needs, making off-grid living more achievable.

Off-grid earth-covered homes also benefit from their natural insulation and temperature regulation, which reduces the need for energy-hungry heating and cooling systems. With the right design and planning, these homes can generate all the power and water they need, allowing homeowners to live sustainably and independently.

Case Study: The Johnson Family's Off-Grid Earth-Covered Home

To see how all of these elements come together, let's take a look at the **Johnson family**, who decided to build an off-grid earth-covered home in a rural area. Tired of high utility bills and concerned about their environmental impact, they wanted a home that could operate independently of public utilities and provide a more sustainable way of living.

The Johnsons' home was built into a south-facing hillside, taking advantage of the earth's natural insulation and passive solar design to reduce energy needs. They installed solar panels on the exposed sections of their roof to generate electricity, along with a small wind turbine for additional power during the winter months. The combination of solar and wind energy allowed them to generate enough electricity to power their entire home, with surplus energy stored in a battery system for use during cloudy or windless days.

For heating and cooling, the Johnsons opted for a geothermal system, which provided consistent, energy-efficient temperature control throughout the year. Their home stayed cool in the summer and warm in the winter with minimal energy use, thanks to the geothermal heat pump working in tandem with the home's natural insulation.

To achieve water independence, the Johnsons installed a rainwater harvesting system that collected and filtered rainwater from their roof. They also implemented a greywater recycling system, allowing them to reuse water from showers, sinks, and laundry for irrigation and toilet flushing. Between these two systems, they were able to meet nearly all of their water needs without relying on municipal supplies.

After going off-grid, the Johnsons found that not only did they drastically reduce their environmental footprint, but they also experienced significant financial savings. Without utility bills for electricity, heating, or water, their monthly expenses dropped to a fraction of what they had been in their previous home. The peace of mind that came with living sustainably—and independently—was a bonus they hadn't expected.

Their off-grid earth-covered home became a model of how renewable energy, smart design, and natural resources can work together to create a self-sustaining, eco-friendly lifestyle.

Conclusion: Renewable energy systems, when paired with the energy efficiency of earth-covered homes, offer a path to truly sustainable living. Whether it's solar panels, wind turbines, geothermal systems, or water recycling, these homes can integrate cutting-edge technologies to reduce their environmental impact and even operate entirely off-grid. The Johnson family's experience shows that with the right planning and design, it's possible to live comfortably, sustainably, and independently.

Now that we've seen how earth-covered homes can integrate renewable energy for maximum efficiency, let's take a closer look at how these homes offer long-term financial and energy savings, proving that sustainability can also be smart for your wallet.

Long-Term Savings on Maintenance

One of the most appealing aspects of earth-covered homes—beyond their energy efficiency and environmental benefits—is how little maintenance they require over time. Homeowners are often surprised to learn that these homes, with their natural insulation and unique construction, demand far less upkeep than traditional houses. Whether it's the durability of the materials, the lack of exposure to the elements, or their resilience to natural disasters, earth-covered homes provide significant long-term savings when it comes to maintenance.

Let's explore why earth-covered homes are not only easier to maintain but also more cost-effective in the long run.

1. Earth-Covered Homes Require Less Maintenance Than Traditional Homes

In a traditional home, maintenance can be a constant and sometimes expensive concern. Roofs need regular repairs or replacement every 20 to 30 years. Siding can warp, crack, or require repainting. Windows need to be resealed, and the exterior is constantly exposed to the wear and tear of wind, rain, and sun.

Earth-covered homes, by contrast, are protected by the earth itself, which means much of the structure is shielded from the elements. With a large portion of the home covered by soil or built into a hillside, the roof, walls, and exterior surfaces don't suffer the same level of exposure as traditional homes. The earth acts as a natural barrier, protecting the home from rain, wind, snow, and sun.

Roofing and siding are two of the most common maintenance headaches for homeowners, but with an earth-covered home, these worries are drastically reduced. Instead of a traditional roof that needs to be repaired or replaced over time, many earth-covered homes have **green roofs**—roofs covered in plants and soil. These green roofs not only provide additional insulation and improve energy efficiency but also last far longer than a conventional roof. Maintenance usually involves occasional weeding or planting, but compared to the cost of replacing a roof, it's a minor task.

Similarly, with most of the walls either underground or bermed with earth, there's no need to worry about siding maintenance. The earth protects the structure, and there's no exterior painting or sealing required. As a result, homeowners save both time and money on the routine upkeep that traditional homes demand.

2. Resilience to Natural Disasters

One of the hidden benefits of earth-covered homes is their **resilience to natural disasters**. Traditional homes are vulnerable to the forces of nature—wildfires, floods, hurricanes, and earthquakes can all cause significant damage. Earth-covered homes, on the other hand, are uniquely suited to withstand these events thanks to their design and the natural protection provided by the earth.

- **Fires:** Earth-covered homes are naturally resistant to wildfires because the earth and green roofs do not burn. Even in areas prone to wildfires, earth-covered homes provide a level of safety that traditional homes simply cannot match. While a wooden roof on a traditional home could ignite during a fire, the soil and plants on a green roof are much less likely to catch fire, offering greater peace of mind to homeowners living in fire-prone regions.
- **Floods:** Homes built into the earth, especially those on slopes or hillsides, have natural drainage systems that help protect against flooding. Water is more likely to be absorbed by the surrounding soil or channeled away from the home by berms and landscaping. Traditional homes, with their exposed foundations and basements, are more prone to water damage during heavy rain or floods.
- **Earthquakes:** Because earth-covered homes are often built with **reinforced concrete** and other sturdy materials, they are highly resistant to earthquakes. The surrounding

earth provides additional stability, helping the structure absorb and distribute seismic forces more effectively than a traditional above-ground home. This makes them ideal in regions where earthquakes are a concern.

- **High Winds and Storms:** The low profile and thick walls of an earth-covered home also offer excellent protection from high winds and severe storms. Unlike traditional homes with exposed roofs and walls that can be damaged or destroyed by strong winds, earth-covered homes are sheltered by the very land they are built into. This makes them less vulnerable to storm damage, further reducing maintenance costs over time.

3. The Lifespan of Materials and Structures

Earth-covered homes are built to last. The materials used in their construction—such as **rammed earth**, **concrete**, and **stone**—have extremely long lifespans compared to the wood and composite materials often used in traditional home construction. These durable materials not only contribute to the home's structural integrity but also require minimal upkeep, adding to the long-term savings.

Rammed earth walls, for example, can last for hundreds of years with little to no maintenance. The compacted earth used to build these walls is incredibly strong, and since the material is naturally abundant and eco-friendly, it's a sustainable choice as well. Similarly, concrete used in earth-covered homes provides exceptional strength and durability, requiring far fewer repairs than traditional building materials.

In addition to the longevity of the materials, the structure of an earth-covered home is designed to be **low-maintenance**. With the exterior of the home protected by the earth, there's less exposure to the elements, reducing the likelihood of damage and wear over time. The home's design works with the natural landscape, offering stability and durability that far exceeds the average lifespan of traditional homes.

4. Cost Comparisons Between Upkeep for Traditional and Earth-Covered Homes

Let's take a closer look at how these long-term maintenance savings translate into actual costs. Maintaining a traditional home can be expensive—between roof repairs, siding replacements, and routine painting or sealing, homeowners can easily spend thousands of dollars on upkeep every few years. Earth-covered homes, on the other hand, drastically reduce these costs.

- **Roof Maintenance:** A traditional roof can cost anywhere from $5,000 to $15,000 (or more) to replace, depending on the size and materials. With a green roof or an earth-covered home, the need for roof replacement is virtually eliminated. Green roofs, with their layers of soil and vegetation, have much longer lifespans than conventional roofs, and maintenance usually involves simple tasks like reseeding or trimming plants.
- **Siding and Exterior:** Maintaining the exterior of a tradi-

tional home can also add up, with repainting or resealing costing thousands of dollars every few years. In an earth-covered home, the walls are either protected by the earth or built from durable materials like rammed earth or concrete, which require no repainting or resealing. This results in substantial savings over the lifetime of the home.

- **Repairs After Natural Disasters:** In the event of a natural disaster, the costs to repair a traditional home can be over-whelming. Roofs blown off in hurricanes, walls damaged by high winds, or foundations flooded during storms can cost tens of thousands of dollars to repair. Earth-covered homes, with their natural disaster resilience, face far fewer risks and repair costs in these situations, providing further long-term savings.

Personal Narrative: A Builder's Experience Maintaining Earth-Covered Homes

Let me share a story from my friend **Mark**, a builder who's worked on earth-covered homes for over 30 years. Mark started his career building traditional homes, but after his first earth-covered project, he was hooked. The simplicity and sustainability of these homes were undeniable, but what truly impressed him was how little maintenance they required over time.

Mark often checks in with the homeowners he's built for, and he's always struck by how rarely they call him for repairs. One couple he built a home for nearly 20 years ago still hasn't had to replace their green roof—other than the occasional weeding and replanting, it's held up beautifully. The bermed walls are just as sturdy as the day they were built, and the family has never had to deal with the leaks or cracks that are so common in traditional homes.

One of Mark's proudest moments was when a massive storm rolled through the area, causing significant damage to the nearby traditional homes. But the earth-covered homes he had built remained untouched, their natural protection keeping them safe and dry. Seeing the difference firsthand confirmed to Mark that these homes weren't just eco-friendly—they were built to last.

Conclusion: Earth-covered homes are more than just energy-efficient and environmentally friendly—they offer substantial long-term savings on maintenance. With fewer repairs, greater resilience to natural disasters, and materials that last for decades, these homes outshine traditional houses when it comes to durability and upkeep. For homeowners looking for a low-maintenance, high-reward living solution, earth-covered homes are an investment that pays off over time.

Now that we know the practical benefits of earth-covered homes, it's time to dive into the exciting part—*designing* your earth-covered dream home. Let's explore how to create a home that blends seamlessly with the landscape and reflects your personal style.

5

Designing an Earth-Covered Home

I magine a house where every room feels like an extension of nature—where the lines between indoors and outdoors blur. Picture yourself waking up to the sound of birds, with sunlight streaming in through wide windows that open to green hills or lush gardens. In an earth-covered home, this connection to the environment isn't just an idea—it's the reality of daily living. These homes are designed to blend harmoniously with their surroundings, creating spaces that are both beautiful and functional. Let's explore how to design an earth-covered home that not only looks stunning but also works seamlessly with the natural world.

Blending with the Environment

One of the most exciting aspects of designing an earth-covered home is the opportunity to create a space that feels deeply connected to the environment. Unlike traditional homes that often dominate the landscape, earth-covered homes are designed to harmonize with it. The result is a home that feels as though it naturally belongs in its setting, with each room offering a sense of peace and balance.

1. Designing Homes That Harmonize with Their Natural Surroundings

The first step in designing an earth-covered home is understanding how to make it a part of the landscape. These homes aren't just built *on* the land—they are integrated *into* it. By working with the natural contours of the land, such as hillsides, valleys, or flat plains, an earth-covered home can be nestled into the terrain, blending seamlessly with the environment.

Designing with the land in mind often means allowing the landscape to guide the shape and orientation of the home. For example, a home built into the side of a hill might feature an open south-facing façade, allowing sunlight to flood the interior, while the back and sides of the house are buried in the earth for insulation and privacy. This approach not only creates a visually stunning home but also maximizes energy efficiency and comfort.

It's all about finding the balance between architecture and nature. By using the land as a design element, you create a home that works with the environment rather than against it. The result is a home that feels like a natural extension of the landscape.

2. Principles of Biophilic Design

At the heart of earth-covered home design is the concept of **biophilic design**, a philosophy that seeks to connect people with nature through architecture. Biophilic design focuses on incorporating natural elements—like light, air, water, and vegetation—into the home in ways that enhance both the beauty of the space and the well-being of its occupants.

Earth-covered homes are an ideal canvas for biophilic design. Here's how these principles can be applied:

- **Views of Nature:** Large, strategically placed windows offer expansive views of the surrounding landscape, bringing the outside world into the home. Whether it's a forest, a garden, or a hillside, these views help foster a sense of calm and connection to nature.
- **Natural Materials:** By using materials like stone, wood, and soil, earth-covered homes maintain a close connection to the environment. These materials not only look beautiful but also create a sense of continuity between the indoor and outdoor spaces.
- **Water Elements:** Biophilic design often includes water features, such as ponds, fountains, or streams. In an earth-covered home, these elements can be integrated into the landscape, enhancing the overall tranquility of the space.
- **Indoor Plants and Green Spaces:** Bringing plants into the home is a simple yet powerful way to connect with nature. Indoor gardens, green walls, or even small courtyards can transform an earth-covered home into a living, breathing ecosystem.

By embracing biophilic design, an earth-covered home becomes more than just a place to live—it becomes a space that nurtures both body and mind. Studies have shown that living in environments that incorporate natural elements can reduce stress, improve mood, and even enhance cognitive function. So, designing a home that connects you to nature isn't just good for the planet—it's good for you, too.

3. Using Natural Light and Ventilation to Enhance Livability

One of the most critical aspects of earth-covered home design is making sure that the interior feels light, airy, and inviting. Because these homes are often partially or fully buried, it's essential to design them in a way that maximizes natural light and ventilation. The goal is to create a space that feels open and connected to the outdoors, even if much of the structure is underground.

- **Maximizing Natural Light:** The use of large, south-facing windows is a hallmark of earth-covered home design. These windows allow sunlight to flood the interior, warming the home naturally in the winter and creating a bright, cheerful atmosphere. In the summer, carefully designed overhangs or green roofs provide shade, preventing the home from overheating. **Skylights** and **light wells** can also be incorporated into the design to bring natural light into rooms that are fully or partially underground.
- **Ventilation for Comfort:** Proper ventilation is key to ensuring that an earth-covered home remains comfortable throughout the year. Natural ventilation systems, such as

cross-ventilation (where windows or vents are placed on opposite sides of a room to allow air to flow through) can help keep the air fresh and cool. Some designs even use **earth tubes**, which are underground pipes that draw in cool air during the summer and warm air during the winter, reducing the need for mechanical heating and cooling systems.

By focusing on natural light and ventilation, you can create an earth-covered home that feels spacious, breathable, and full of life. It's about ensuring that the home remains connected to the natural rhythms of the day and the seasons, making it a comfortable place to live no matter the time of year.

4. Incorporating Natural Elements Like Rock and Soil Into the Home

Another distinctive feature of earth-covered homes is the way they incorporate natural elements like **rock**, **soil**, and **vegetation** into the design. These materials aren't just used for structural purposes—they become part of the aesthetic and the experience of living in the home.

- **Rock and Stone:** In many earth-covered homes, **exposed rock walls** or **natural stone features** are used to create a sense of continuity between the indoor and outdoor spaces. These elements add texture and warmth to the interior, while also emphasizing the home's connection to the earth. Whether it's a stone fireplace or a rocky wall that's part of the hillside the home is built into, these natural elements become focal points within the design.

- **Green Roofs and Berms:** Green roofs, covered with soil and plants, are not only practical for insulation and water management but also serve as an extension of the surrounding landscape. These living roofs can be planted with native grasses, wildflowers, or even small shrubs, creating a seamless transition between the home and its natural environment.
- **Earth Floors and Clay Walls:** Some earth-covered homes go even further by using **earth floors** or **clay walls**, which not only add a rustic charm but also help regulate humidity and temperature within the home. These natural materials are both sustainable and functional, contributing to the home's overall energy efficiency.

By incorporating these natural elements into the design, you create a home that feels like it's truly part of the landscape. The result is a living space that's both visually stunning and deeply connected to the environment.

Case Study: A Home Nestled Into a Hillside

One of the most inspiring examples of earth-covered home design is the **Sage Hollow House**, a home built into a hillside in the Pacific Northwest. Designed to blend seamlessly with its surroundings, this home uses the landscape itself as part of the architecture.

The home's design takes full advantage of the natural slope of the land. The south-facing side of the house features large windows that overlook a valley, allowing sunlight to pour in throughout the day. The rest of the home is built into the hillside, with earth covering the roof and sides, providing natural insulation and protection from the elements.

Inside, the home is a perfect example of biophilic design. Exposed stone walls, harvested from the site, create a sense of continuity between the indoors and outdoors. A central courtyard, open to the sky, brings light and fresh air into the heart of the home, while the green roof above is planted with native vegetation, helping the home disappear into the landscape.

The homeowners wanted a space that felt deeply connected to nature, and the result is a home where every room offers a view of the surrounding landscape. Whether they're cooking in the kitchen, relaxing in the living room, or soaking in the outdoor tub, they always feel a sense of peace and tranquility that comes from living in harmony with the earth.

Conclusion: Designing an earth-covered home is an opportunity to create a space that feels like part of the natural world. By blending architecture with the environment, incorporating biophilic design principles, and using natural light, ventilation, and materials, you can craft a home that's not only beautiful but also deeply connected to the land. The Sage Hollow House shows what's possible when you let the landscape guide the design, creating a home that's a true extension of nature.

Now that we've explored how to design an earth-covered

home that blends seamlessly with the environment, let's dive into the practical considerations—like site selection and soil conditions—that will set the foundation for your project.

Modern Aesthetics with Earth-Covered Homes

When people think of earth-covered homes, they often imagine something ancient, perhaps primitive—a home dug out of a hillside or resembling a Hobbit-like retreat. But today's earth-covered homes are anything but. In fact, many of them are at the cutting edge of modern design, combining sleek, minimalist aesthetics with the timeless benefits of living in harmony with the earth. Earth-covered homes can be as modern and stylish as any contemporary structure, and in many cases, they offer an even more striking visual impact because of how seamlessly they blend with their surroundings.

Let's dive into how modern aesthetics are not only possible with earth-covered homes but can actually enhance their appeal, combining clean lines, open spaces, and natural materials to create homes that feel both innovative and welcoming.

1. Minimalist Design and How It Fits with Earth Homes

Minimalism is all about simplicity, clean lines, and an uncluttered aesthetic—and it pairs perfectly with earth-covered homes. The philosophy behind minimalist design is to create spaces that feel open and free, using only the essentials to create a peaceful, functional living environment. This mindset fits seamlessly with the concept of earth-covered homes, which are built to integrate with nature rather than dominate it.

An earth-covered home naturally lends itself to minimalist design because of its **subtle footprint** in the landscape. The architecture is typically low-profile, with many of the structures either below ground or nestled into the earth. This creates a sleek, understated look that eliminates the need for flashy exterior elements.

Inside, minimalist design shines in earth-covered homes because the architecture often focuses on **large, open spaces** that flow into one another. These homes are often designed with fewer walls, allowing for a sense of openness that feels expansive yet connected to the natural world outside. The minimalist approach avoids unnecessary ornamentation, instead letting the beauty of natural light and materials take center stage.

By focusing on function and simplicity, minimalist design in an earth-covered home can feel calming and grounding. With less clutter and fewer distractions, the home becomes a retreat—a space to escape the busyness of life and reconnect with nature in its purest form.

2. Creating Open, Spacious Interiors

One of the most common misconceptions about earth-covered homes is that they might feel cramped or confined. After all, much of the home is surrounded by earth, which leads some people to think the interiors would be small or dark. However, the reality is quite the opposite. Many earth-covered homes are designed with **open, spacious interiors** that feel airy and expansive.

The key to creating open spaces in an earth-covered home is thoughtful design. By using **large, south-facing windows**, **skylights**, and **light wells**, designers can flood the home with natural light, making the interiors feel bright and inviting. This natural light creates a sense of openness, even in spaces that are partially underground.

The **floor plan** of an earth-covered home often emphasizes a flow between rooms, with fewer walls dividing the space. This not only creates a more modern, open-concept feel but also allows for better use of natural light and ventilation. With fewer barriers, the home feels larger and more connected to the surrounding landscape, giving it a sense of seamless continuity.

Vaulted ceilings or **sunken living rooms** are popular design choices in modern earth-covered homes. These elements add a feeling of spaciousness by drawing the eye upward or creating depth in the floor plan. The result is a home that feels expansive, despite being surrounded by the earth.

3. Use of Natural Materials Like Stone and Wood for a Warm, Inviting Atmosphere

While modern design often focuses on clean lines and open

spaces, it's important that earth-covered homes still feel warm and welcoming. This is where **natural materials** like stone and wood come into play. These materials not only tie the home to its natural surroundings but also add a sense of warmth that balances the minimalist aesthetic.

Incorporating **natural stone** into the design—whether it's through exposed rock walls, a stone fireplace, or stone flooring—brings a grounding, earthy quality to the home. The texture and color of stone contrast beautifully with smooth, minimalist surfaces, adding visual interest and warmth to the interior.

Similarly, **wood** is an excellent material for creating a cozy, inviting atmosphere in an earth-covered home. Whether used for beams, flooring, or cabinetry, wood adds warmth and texture that softens the sleekness of modern design. The grain and natural imperfections of wood complement the clean lines of minimalist architecture, creating a harmonious blend of modernity and nature.

The combination of stone and wood with modern design elements creates a home that feels contemporary yet timeless. The natural materials invite the outdoors in, making the home feel like an extension of the landscape. And, importantly, these materials help the home avoid the cold, sterile feeling that can sometimes come with modern design.

4. How to Make Earth-Covered Homes Look Modern, Not Primitive

One of the challenges with earth-covered homes is ensuring that they look modern rather than primitive. While the idea of building a home into the earth might seem old-fashioned, contemporary design elements can transform these homes into sleek, futuristic spaces that feel anything but rustic.

Here are a few ways to achieve a modern look in an earth-covered home:

- **Clean Lines and Simple Forms:** Focus on clean, geometric lines in the design of the home. This minimalist approach creates a modern aesthetic that contrasts with the organic shapes of the natural landscape. Think of straight-edged windows, flat roofs, and angular walls that offer a sleek contrast to the soft curves of the earth.
- **Neutral Color Palette:** Using a neutral color palette—shades of white, gray, beige, and black—creates a sophisticated, modern look. The natural colors of the surrounding earth and stone will bring warmth and texture to the space, while the clean palette keeps the home feeling modern and uncluttered.
- **Glass and Metal Accents:** Incorporating modern materials like glass and metal can elevate the design of an earth-covered home. **Floor-to-ceiling glass windows** make a bold statement, allowing natural light to pour in and offering stunning views of the landscape. **Metal accents**—whether in light fixtures, furniture, or railings—can add a sleek, industrial touch that contrasts beautifully with the home's natural materials.
- **Smart Home Technology:** Incorporating smart home technology into the design is another way to give an earth-

covered home a modern edge. From automated lighting systems to energy-efficient climate control, integrating technology helps modernize the home's functionality and enhances the overall living experience.

By focusing on these design elements, earth-covered homes can be transformed from rustic, cave-like dwellings into modern architectural masterpieces that feel current and cutting-edge.

Story: An Architect's Approach to Balancing Modern Aesthetics with Sustainability

Architect **Lisa Greene** is known for her innovative designs that blend modern aesthetics with sustainable living. When she was approached by a family looking to build an earth-covered home on their property, they had one key request: they wanted the home to be *modern*, not rustic.

Lisa loved the challenge. She knew that building an earth-covered home would naturally lend itself to sustainability, with its energy-efficient design and low environmental impact. But her goal was to make this home feel sleek and contemporary, a space that would be just as at home in a city as it was in the countryside.

To achieve this, Lisa focused on clean lines and open spaces. She designed the home with a **minimalist aesthetic**, using large, unbroken surfaces and simple forms. The windows were massive, floor-to-ceiling panes that let in natural light and offered panoramic views of the surrounding landscape. The interior featured **exposed stone walls**, carefully balanced with warm wood floors and neutral-toned furnishings, giving the home a sophisticated yet earthy feel.

Lisa also incorporated **smart home technology** throughout the house, allowing the family to control lighting, temperature, and security with a single touch. The home's design was futuristic, but it also honored the natural landscape by blending into the hillside, with a green roof that made the house nearly invisible from a distance.

The family loved the result. They had a home that felt as modern as any urban loft, but with all the benefits of sustainable, earth-covered living. Lisa's approach demonstrated that you don't have to choose between modern design and sustainability—you can have both.

Conclusion: Modern aesthetics and earth-covered homes aren't mutually exclusive. With thoughtful design choices, minimalist principles, and the use of natural materials, you can create a home that's both contemporary and deeply connected to the earth. Whether you're using stone and wood to bring warmth to your space or incorporating sleek, modern lines to contrast with the natural landscape, earth-covered homes offer a unique opportunity to blend style with sustainability.

Now that we've explored how modern design can elevate your earth-covered home, let's dive into site selection and the critical role that soil and land conditions play in bringing your dream home to life

The Future of Earth-Covered Design

As we look to the future of architecture, earth-covered homes are positioned to play a significant role in how we think about sustainable living. These homes, which are already celebrated for their energy efficiency and environmental benefits, are evolving to meet the needs of a changing world. With advancements in technology, a growing emphasis on sustainability, and the increasing need for innovative housing solutions in urban environments, the next generation of earth-covered homes will push the boundaries of design and function.

Let's explore some of the futuristic possibilities for earth-covered homes, from smart homes that manage themselves to underground eco-cities that redefine urban living.

1. Futuristic, Innovative Earth-Covered Homes

The earth-covered homes of tomorrow will likely be far more sophisticated than the ones we see today. As architects and designers experiment with new materials, construction techniques, and technologies, these homes are set to become even more efficient, aesthetically striking, and adaptable.

3D printing is one exciting development that could revolutionize the construction of earth-covered homes. This technology allows builders to create custom-designed homes with complex shapes that would be difficult or expensive to achieve using traditional methods. Imagine a home that is not only built into the landscape but also designed to mimic the natural contours of the surrounding earth. With 3D printing, homes could be printed directly on-site using local materials like soil and clay, drastically reducing construction waste and carbon emissions.

Moreover, as materials science advances, we may see the rise of **self-healing materials** that can repair themselves over time, reducing the need for maintenance. These materials, combined with the natural durability of earth-covered structures, could extend the lifespan of homes even further, making them more resilient to environmental wear and tear.

The futuristic design of earth-covered homes will continue to focus on blending with the landscape while incorporating cutting-edge features that push the boundaries of what's possible in architecture. These homes will not just be functional—they will also be works of art, seamlessly integrated into the natural world.

2. Integrating Technology Into the Design: Smart Homes and AI Energy Management

As we move into the future, technology will become an integral part of earth-covered home design, transforming these homes into **smart homes** that optimize energy use, comfort, and sustainability.

One of the most promising innovations is the integration of **AI-powered energy management systems**. These systems can monitor and adjust a home's energy consumption in real-time, ensuring that the home operates at maximum efficiency. For instance, AI could adjust heating, cooling, and lighting based on weather conditions, time of day, and even the homeowner's daily routines. By analyzing data, the system can anticipate energy needs and make adjustments to reduce waste, saving both energy and money.

Smart appliances and **automated systems** will also play a major role in future earth-covered homes. From intelligent lighting that adapts to natural daylight to smart thermostats that optimize indoor temperatures based on outside conditions, these homes will be designed to function with minimal human input. Sensors embedded in the home's infrastructure could monitor everything from humidity levels to structural integrity, alerting homeowners to potential issues before they become costly problems.

Imagine a home that automatically adjusts its energy usage based on real-time data, opens or closes windows for natural ventilation, and manages water conservation systems based on weather forecasts. This level of integration would not only make earth-covered homes more convenient and efficient but would also ensure they remain at the forefront of sustainable living.

3. Urban Applications and High-Density Earth-Covered Housing

As cities continue to grow and space becomes more limited, there is a pressing need for innovative housing solutions that can accommodate high-density populations while minimizing environmental impact. **Earth-covered homes**, with their natural insulation and energy efficiency, offer a compelling solution for urban living. But what does the future hold for these homes in an urban context?

In densely populated cities, **high-density earth-covered housing** could become a reality. These structures could be built partially underground or incorporated into existing green spaces, reducing the visible footprint of buildings while maximizing the use of land. Urban planners could design **multi-level, earth-covered complexes**, where each level is embedded into the landscape, creating a vertical community that's energy-efficient and environmentally conscious.

These urban earth-covered homes wouldn't just be isolated structures; they could be integrated into **green infrastructure networks** that include parks, green roofs, and public spaces. By building homes beneath parks or other green areas, cities could maintain public green spaces while providing much-needed housing. This approach would reduce urban sprawl and help combat the **urban heat island effect**, all while offering residents a connection to nature that's often missing in city life.

The future of earth-covered homes in urban environments could also include **underground transportation hubs** or **shared energy grids** that connect entire neighborhoods. This integration of housing and infrastructure would allow for more sustainable and efficient cities, where natural resources are conserved, and urban spaces are reimagined.

4. Sustainable Luxury Homes Built Into the Earth

For those looking for both sustainability and luxury, the future of earth-covered homes holds exciting possibilities. **Sustainable luxury** is a growing trend in the real estate market, as more high-end homeowners seek eco-friendly designs that don't compromise on comfort or aesthetics. Earth-covered homes, with their ability to merge environmental responsibility with cutting-edge design, are a perfect fit for this niche.

Luxury earth-covered homes could feature expansive, open interiors with panoramic views of the surrounding landscape, achieved through carefully designed glass walls and skylights. **Infinity pools** integrated into the earth's contours, **indoor gardens,** and **outdoor terraces** that blend seamlessly with green roofs are just a few of the features that could define these homes. Natural materials like reclaimed wood, stone, and clay could be paired with high-end finishes to create spaces that feel luxurious yet grounded in nature.

Sustainability would remain a core principle, with smart home technologies managing energy consumption, **geothermal heating and cooling systems** ensuring year-round comfort, and **rainwater harvesting systems** supporting self-sufficiency. These homes would offer the ultimate combination of luxury and environmental stewardship, appealing to homeowners who want to live in harmony with the planet without sacrificing modern conveniences.

Example: A Conceptual Design for a Futuristic Underground Eco-City

To see the potential of earth-covered homes on a grand scale, consider the conceptual design for an underground **eco-city** called **Terra Vitae**, envisioned by a group of forward-thinking architects and urban planners. Terra Vitae represents the future of sustainable urban living, where entire cities are built below ground, taking advantage of the earth's natural insulating properties while preserving the surface for agriculture, recreation, and biodiversity.

In Terra Vitae, buildings would be partially or fully underground, designed to minimize energy use through **passive solar design**, **geothermal systems**, and **AI-driven energy management**. The surface above the city would remain largely undeveloped, providing vast green spaces for farming and wildlife, all while supporting the city's needs. Rooftops of underground buildings would become community parks, gardens, and forests, allowing residents to enjoy the benefits of green space without sacrificing valuable land.

Transportation in Terra Vitae would rely on electric vehicles and underground tunnels, reducing air pollution and traffic congestion. Energy would be generated through a combination of **solar panels**, **wind turbines**, and **geothermal plants**, with excess energy stored in batteries for future use. Water would be conserved through **rainwater harvesting** and **greywater recycling systems**, making the city nearly self-sufficient.

Residents of Terra Vitae would live in modern, luxury earth-covered homes that offer all the amenities of a contemporary urban lifestyle while contributing to the city's sustainability goals. The concept of Terra Vitae challenges our traditional ideas of what cities can be, showing us a future where urban life is in perfect balance with nature.

Conclusion: The future of earth-covered homes is bright, filled with possibilities for innovation, sustainability, and modern design. From smart homes that manage themselves to luxury dwellings that blend effortlessly with the landscape, earth-covered homes are poised to redefine how we think about living in harmony with the planet. As urban populations grow and environmental challenges intensify, earth-covered homes offer a path forward, providing both beauty and sustainability for generations to come.

Before you start planning your own earth-covered home, there are key considerations to make about location, soil conditions, and site selection. Let's explore these practical aspects to ensure your dream home is built on a solid foundation.

6

Site Selection and Soil Considerations

The success of your earth-covered home starts with what's beneath your feet—choosing the right site can make or break the project. While the design of your home is important, the land it sits on is equally critical. Selecting the right site ensures that your home not only functions efficiently but also lasts for generations. Let's dive into the essential factors to consider when evaluating your land for an earth-covered home and how those decisions will impact everything from energy efficiency to long-term costs.

Evaluating Your Land

Before any construction can begin on your earth-covered home, it's crucial to thoroughly evaluate the land you're building on. The right site can optimize your home's energy efficiency, reduce costs, and ensure the structure is well-protected from environmental challenges. By carefully analyzing factors like slope, orientation, drainage, and climate, you can design a home that works in harmony with its natural surroundings.

1. Importance of Proper Land Evaluation Before Construction

The process of evaluating land for an earth-covered home is different from that of a traditional build. Earth-covered homes interact directly with the environment around them, which means every detail of the landscape will influence how your home performs. For instance, a hillside may offer ideal conditions for building into the earth, reducing energy needs and excavation costs. However, a poorly chosen site with drainage issues or weak soil could lead to expensive problems down the road.

Before construction begins, a **site analysis** should be performed to assess the land's characteristics. This analysis will include an evaluation of the soil type, drainage capacity, wind patterns, and solar exposure. It's also important to work with professionals who understand earth-covered home construction and can identify potential issues before they arise. Taking the time to properly evaluate the land upfront will save you time, money, and headaches in the long run.

2. Key Factors: Slope, Orientation, Drainage, and Natural Wind Breaks

Slope and Topography

One of the most critical factors in choosing a site for your earth-covered home is the **slope** of the land. A sloped site is ideal because it allows you to build into the earth, using the natural contour of the land to your advantage. Homes built into a hillside can benefit from better insulation and temperature regulation, as the surrounding earth helps maintain stable indoor temperatures.

The slope also helps with **water drainage**, directing rainwater away from the home and reducing the risk of flooding. Additionally, working with the natural slope can lower excavation costs, as less earth needs to be moved to create the desired structure.

Orientation

The orientation of your home is another key factor. Ideally, an earth-covered home should be positioned with its main windows and living areas facing **south** to maximize passive solar heating in the winter months. South-facing homes receive the most sunlight during the colder months when the sun is lower in the sky, allowing for natural warmth and reducing the need for additional heating.

In the summer, when the sun is higher, proper orientation can prevent overheating by using **overhangs**, **berms**, or vegetation to shade the home. This balance of sunlight and shade keeps the home comfortable year-round and drastically reduces energy consumption.

Drainage

Good **drainage** is essential for any earth-covered home. Because the home is surrounded by soil, managing water flow around the structure is crucial to prevent moisture buildup, leaks, and long-term damage. A site with natural drainage—such as a sloping hillside—helps keep water away from the home's foundation.

When evaluating a site, it's important to look for areas where water naturally pools, as these spots may indicate poor drainage. Working with the topography to create natural water pathways, as well as incorporating drainage systems like **French drains**, ensures that water moves away from the home rather than toward it.

Natural Wind Breaks

Another important consideration is **wind exposure**. Homes built in areas with strong winds can experience greater heat loss, which undermines the energy efficiency of an earth-covered design. Choosing a site with natural wind breaks—like trees, hills, or other landscape features—can help shield your home from harsh winds.

For example, building on the **leeward side of a hill** (the side protected from prevailing winds) can significantly reduce the wind's impact on the structure. Natural wind breaks help maintain a more stable indoor temperature, further reducing energy costs and improving the overall comfort of the home.

3. Climate Considerations (Hot vs. Cold Regions and Humid-

ity)

The **climate** in which you're building plays a major role in the design and functionality of your earth-covered home. Earth-covered homes are highly adaptable, but your approach will differ depending on whether you're building in a hot, cold, or humid region.

Cold Regions

In colder climates, earth-covered homes are especially beneficial due to their ability to retain heat. A well-designed earth-covered home will take advantage of **passive solar heating**, using large south-facing windows to capture the sun's heat during the day. The earth surrounding the home acts as an insulating barrier, keeping the heat in and reducing the need for mechanical heating systems.

In these regions, the home's roof and walls will also need to be well-insulated to prevent heat loss. Additionally, ensuring proper drainage is critical in cold areas, as melting snow or ice can lead to moisture problems if not managed correctly.

Hot Regions

In hot climates, the goal is to keep the home cool. Here, the earth-covered design works to your advantage by naturally **regulating indoor temperatures**. The earth surrounding the home prevents excessive heat from penetrating the walls, while proper orientation and shading minimize solar gain.

In these areas, using ventilation systems to encourage airflow, combined with thick walls to block out heat, can create a naturally cool living space. Homes in hot regions may also benefit from **green roofs**, which further insulate the home and help reduce temperatures inside.

Humid Regions

In humid climates, moisture control becomes the primary concern. While earth-covered homes are great at temperature regulation, high humidity can lead to condensation and moisture buildup if not properly managed. To prevent this, it's important to incorporate **waterproofing measures** like drainage membranes and vapor barriers.

Ventilation is also key in humid regions to prevent mold and mildew. Homes should be designed with cross-ventilation to ensure good air circulation, and **dehumidifiers** may be necessary in areas with extremely high moisture levels.

4. Working With Topography to Reduce Excavation Costs

One of the major advantages of building an earth-covered home is the ability to work with the natural **topography** of the land. By using the landscape to your advantage, you can significantly reduce the costs associated with excavation and construction.

For example, building into a hillside naturally provides the earth cover needed for insulation, which means less earth needs to be moved. This not only saves on excavation costs but also minimizes the environmental impact of the build. In flat areas, berming soil around the home can achieve similar results, though this may require more material.

By selecting a site with favorable topography, you can keep construction costs down while still enjoying the benefits of earth-covered living.

Story: A Builder's Experience Selecting the Perfect Hillside for a Passive Solar Home

Several years ago, a builder named **David** was tasked with creating a passive solar, earth-covered home for a family in a rural area. The family had found a piece of land they loved, but the terrain was challenging—steep in some areas and flat in others. David knew that the success of the project hinged on selecting the perfect spot on the property.

After thoroughly evaluating the land, David found an ideal hillside with a gentle south-facing slope. The slope was perfect for the passive solar design, allowing for large windows to face south and capture the sun's warmth during the winter. The hill itself provided natural insulation, and its shape helped direct water away from the home, eliminating concerns about drainage.

By building into the hillside, David was able to minimize excavation costs, use the natural topography for insulation, and take full advantage of passive solar heating. The result was a home that blended seamlessly into the landscape while staying warm in the winter and cool in the summer—all with minimal energy use.

David's experience underscores the importance of choosing the right site. In this case, the hillside made all the difference, turning a potentially challenging plot of land into the perfect location for a sustainable, energy-efficient home.

Conclusion:

Selecting the right site for your earth-covered home is critical to ensuring its long-term success. From evaluating the slope and orientation to understanding the climate and drainage, proper site selection sets the foundation for an efficient, resilient, and comfortable home. By working with the natural landscape, you can reduce costs, improve energy efficiency, and create a home that's truly in harmony with the earth.

Now that you've chosen the perfect site, it's time to dive into the next step: mastering the building techniques that will bring your earth-covered home to life. Let's explore the construction methods that make these homes so unique and sustainable.

Understanding Soil Types

The foundation of any successful earth-covered home starts, quite literally, in the soil. While the design and site selection are crucial, the type of soil on your land can significantly impact the stability, longevity, and success of your home. Understanding soil composition and its interaction with your earth-covered structure is vital to avoid problems down the line. In this chapter, we'll explore the different soil types, why soil testing is essential, and how to manage soil stability and moisture for a safe and sustainable home.

Soil Testing and How Soil Composition Affects Construction

Before breaking ground on an earth-covered home, one of the most important steps is conducting a **soil test**. This test provides critical information about the soil's composition, strength, and drainage capacity, all of which affect the construction and stability of your home. Soil that is too loose, prone to water retention, or lacking in stability can cause significant issues during and after construction, leading to settling, cracking, or water infiltration.

A **geotechnical engineer** or soil specialist typically performs the soil test, drilling into the earth and taking samples to analyze the content and properties of the soil at various depths. This analysis will help determine if the soil on your site is suitable for construction or if you need to implement additional measures, like soil stabilization or drainage systems.

Why is soil testing essential?

- **Foundation Strength:** The strength of your home's foundation depends heavily on the soil's ability to bear the weight of the structure. Weak soils can lead to shifting foundations or even structural failure over time.
- **Drainage and Water Management:** Some soils retain water more than others, increasing the risk of water infiltration or damage. Understanding how water moves through your soil is crucial for designing proper drainage systems.
- **Stability:** Earth-covered homes rely on the stability of the surrounding soil to remain structurally sound. Unstable soils may shift or erode, compromising the safety of your

home.

Once the soil test is complete, the results will guide the rest of your planning process, helping you make decisions about the type of foundation, drainage solutions, and even the placement of your home on the site.

Clay, Sand, Silt, and Loam: Which Soils Are Best?

Not all soil types are created equal when it comes to construction, especially for earth-covered homes. Understanding the different types of soil and how they interact with moisture and pressure is key to ensuring your home remains safe and stable for years to come.

Let's break down the four major soil types and which ones work best for earth-covered homes:

1. Clay

Clay is a fine-grained soil that has the ability to hold large amounts of water. While clay is extremely stable when dry, it expands when wet and contracts as it dries out, making it prone to **shrink-swell** cycles. This characteristic can create problems for construction, as the expansion and contraction can lead to foundation cracks and shifting structures.

Pros:

- Clay has strong cohesion, which can help hold earth-covered walls in place.
- Clay acts as a natural sealant, making it somewhat resistant to water infiltration.

Cons:

- Poor drainage, leading to moisture buildup.
- Prone to expansion and contraction, which can cause

structural damage.

Best Practice:

If your site has a lot of clay, additional measures, such as installing **drainage systems** and using stabilizers (like mixing the clay with gravel or sand), can help mitigate the challenges.

2. Sand

Sand is the opposite of clay—it has large particles that drain water quickly. While sandy soil doesn't retain much moisture, it also lacks the stability that denser soils like clay provide. Sand can easily shift under pressure, making it less than ideal for supporting heavy structures.

Pros:

- Excellent drainage.
- Unlikely to expand or contract with moisture changes.

Cons:

- Poor stability and cohesion, especially under load.
- Tends to shift or erode easily.

Best Practice:

For sites with sandy soil, stabilizing the foundation with **retaining walls**, geotextiles, or gravel can provide additional support.

Compacting the sand and mixing it with other materials can also improve stability.

3. Silt

Silt is a fine-grained soil, similar to clay, but with better drainage characteristics. However, silt can become slippery when wet and tends to compact under pressure, making it prone to **erosion** and **water retention**. It lacks the strength to support a heavy structure without reinforcement.

Pros:

- Fair drainage compared to clay.
- Smooth and easy to work with.

Cons:

- Poor load-bearing capacity.
- Erodes easily when exposed to water.

Best Practice:

Like clay, silt requires careful management of drainage and may need reinforcement with other materials, such as gravel or geotextiles, to ensure stability.

4. Loam

Loam is often considered the best soil for construction because it's a balanced mixture of clay, sand, and silt. It has good drainage, retains some moisture without becoming water-logged, and offers better stability than other soil types.

Pros:

- Balanced drainage and moisture retention.
- Stable under pressure, making it ideal for construction.
- Easier to work with during excavation.

Cons:

- Loam is ideal, but rare—most soils are either clay-heavy, sandy, or silty.

Best Practice:

If you're lucky enough to have loam soil, you may need fewer modifications to the site. However, drainage systems are still important to manage water flow effectively.

Managing Soil Stability and Moisture Levels

Once you understand your soil type, the next step is managing its stability and moisture levels to prevent issues like **erosion**, **foundation shifting**, or **water damage**. Here are some techniques commonly used to improve soil stability and manage moisture around earth-covered homes:

- **Compaction:** Compacted soil is more stable and less likely to shift under the weight of the home. During construction, it's important to compact the soil layers around the home to increase stability.

- **Soil Stabilization:** In areas with poor soil stability (such as sandy or silty soils), adding stabilizing agents like **lime** or **cement** can help improve the load-bearing capacity of the soil. This is especially important for the foundation and walls of earth-covered homes.
- **Drainage Systems:** Effective drainage is crucial for maintaining the structural integrity of an earth-covered home. **French drains** or **drainage membranes** can help direct water away from the foundation, preventing moisture from pooling around the home and causing erosion or structural damage.
- **Retaining Walls:** For homes built into hillsides or steep slopes, retaining walls may be necessary to hold the earth in place and prevent landslides or erosion. These walls help distribute the pressure of the earth more evenly and add stability to the structure.

Proper soil management is essential to ensure the long-term stability and safety of your earth-covered home. By addressing soil stability and moisture from the beginning, you can prevent costly problems later on.

Importance of Retaining Walls and Drainage Systems in Certain Soil Types

Some soil types, particularly those prone to erosion or poor drainage, require additional structural support in the form of **retaining walls** and **drainage systems**. These elements are critical for maintaining the stability of your earth-covered home, especially if your site has steep slopes or experiences heavy rainfall.

Retaining Walls

Retaining walls are designed to support the weight of the earth that surrounds your home, keeping it from collapsing or shifting. In clay-heavy or sandy soils, retaining walls are often necessary to ensure that the soil remains stable. These walls also help manage pressure from the surrounding earth, especially if your home is built into a hillside.

Drainage Systems

Drainage systems are equally important, especially in soils that retain moisture, like clay or silt. Without proper drainage, water can seep into the home, causing structural damage and increasing the risk of mold or mildew. **French drains** or **subsurface drainage systems** help channel water away from the home, preventing water buildup and ensuring that the soil remains stable over time.

Case Study: A Project Delayed Due to Poor Soil Management—

and How They Solved It

A builder, **Rebecca**, once faced a serious delay in an earth-covered home project due to poor soil management. The site had been selected for its beautiful view, but during construction, they discovered that the soil was predominantly silt, which was prone to erosion and water retention. After several heavy rainstorms, the soil began to shift, and cracks appeared in the foundation.

The team had to pause the project and reevaluate the soil. They brought in a geotechnical engineer who recommended several solutions. First, they compacted the soil and added a mixture of gravel to improve stability. Next, they installed a **French drain system** to manage water flow around the home. Finally, retaining walls were added to stabilize the earth around the structure.

While the delay added time and cost to the project, the improvements ensured the long-term stability of the home. After the modifications, the home was completed without further issues, and the homeowners enjoyed a beautiful, safe, and sustainable living space.

Conclusion:

Understanding the type of soil you're working with is a critical part of building an earth-covered home. Whether you're dealing with clay, sand, silt, or loam, proper soil management—through testing, drainage, and stabilization—can prevent problems and ensure the longevity of your home. With the right soil strategy in place, you'll be well on your way to creating a home that's not only sustainable but also safe and resilient.

Now that we've covered the importance of soil, let's explore the building techniques that will bring your earth-covered home to life, from foundation to final touches

Climate-Specific Design Considerations

One of the greatest advantages of earth-covered homes is their adaptability to a wide range of climates. Whether you're building in a hot desert, a snowy mountain region, or a coastal area prone to storms, earth-covered homes can be customized to thrive in extreme environments. However, each climate comes with its own set of challenges, and understanding how to adapt your design accordingly is key to ensuring that your home remains comfortable, energy-efficient, and durable for the long haul.

In this section, we'll explore how to design earth-covered homes that not only survive but excel in harsh climates by focusing on natural light, ventilation, moisture control, and disaster resistance.

1. Adapting Your Home to Extreme Climates (Deserts, Coastal Areas, Snowy Regions)

Designing an earth-covered home in an extreme climate requires more than just good insulation—it requires strategic planning to account for the unique demands of the environment. Here's how to adapt your home to different extreme climates:

Desert Regions:

In desert climates, the primary goal is to keep the home cool during the day and warm at night, as temperature fluctuations can be extreme. Earth-covered homes are ideal for deserts because the earth provides natural insulation that keeps heat out during the day and traps warmth at night. Additionally, the design should focus on **passive cooling techniques**, such as positioning the home to take advantage of prevailing breezes and using thick, insulating walls to reduce heat transfer.

In deserts, minimizing sun exposure is key. **Overhangs, shading devices, and berms** can be used to block direct sunlight during the hottest parts of the day, while courtyards and **reflective materials** can help bounce heat away from the home. By embedding the home into the earth, you also benefit from the cooler underground temperatures, which significantly reduce the need for air conditioning.

Coastal Areas:

Coastal regions often face challenges like **high winds**, **humidity**, and the risk of **flooding**. In these areas, designing an earth-covered home with strong **wind resistance** and proper drainage is essential. For coastal homes, positioning the structure on elevated terrain or incorporating drainage systems is crucial to prevent water damage from storms or rising sea levels.

To protect the home from salt-laden winds, which can corrode materials over time, it's important to choose materials that resist corrosion, like stainless steel or treated wood. Coastal homes should also be designed with a focus on **cross-ventilation** to maintain air quality in humid environments. Large, operable windows positioned to catch sea breezes can help keep the home cool and dry.

Snowy and Cold Regions:

In snowy or mountainous regions, the goal is to maximize heat retention and prevent moisture buildup from snow and ice. Earth-covered homes in cold climates benefit from the insulating properties of the earth, which keeps them warmer than above-ground homes. However, you'll need to carefully manage **snow load** on the roof and ensure proper drainage to prevent ice dams and water damage.

Designing with **passive solar principles** is key in cold climates. Large, south-facing windows will capture the sun's warmth during the day, while overhangs or pergolas can prevent too much heat loss at night. Additionally, using materials with high **thermal mass**—such as stone or concrete—helps absorb heat and release it slowly, keeping the home warm throughout the night.

2. Importance of Natural Light and Ventilation in Varying Environments

Natural light and ventilation are critical for any home, but they become even more important in earth-covered homes, where large portions of the structure are surrounded by soil. Maximizing natural light and airflow ensures that the home feels bright, airy, and healthy, no matter the climate.

Natural Light:

In earth-covered homes, **south-facing windows** are the best way to bring in natural light while taking advantage of passive solar heating. For homes in extreme climates—whether hot or cold—getting the right balance of light is crucial. In hot regions, overhangs or **green roofs** can shade windows during the summer, preventing excess heat from entering the home. In colder climates, unobstructed south-facing windows allow the sun to warm the home throughout the day.

For homes with underground or bermed sections, **skylights** or **light wells** can be used to bring sunlight into the deeper parts of the home. These design features not only brighten the space but also reduce the need for artificial lighting, cutting down on energy use.

Ventilation:

Good **ventilation** is essential for maintaining air quality and comfort in earth-covered homes, especially in humid or wet climates where moisture can accumulate. Ventilation helps regulate indoor temperatures, prevent condensation, and ensure a steady flow of fresh air.

In hot climates, designing for **cross-ventilation** is an effective way to keep the home cool without relying on mechanical air conditioning. By placing windows or vents on opposite sides of the home, you can create a natural airflow that cools the interior. In colder climates, ventilation is important for preventing moisture buildup, especially in bathrooms and kitchens. **Operable windows** and **ventilation systems** with heat recovery capabilities can keep the air fresh while minimizing heat loss.

3. How to Avoid Moisture Problems in Wet Climates (Water-proofing, Ventilation)

Moisture is one of the biggest challenges for earth-covered homes, especially in regions with high rainfall or humidity. Proper moisture management is essential to prevent water damage, mold, and other issues that could compromise the structural integrity of the home.

Waterproofing:

The key to avoiding moisture problems is thorough **water-proofing**. During construction, a variety of waterproofing methods can be employed to protect the home from ground-water or rain infiltration. These include using **waterproof membranes**, **vapor barriers**, and **drainage systems** to direct water away from the home. The foundation and walls should be sealed with durable, waterproof materials that can withstand the pressure of the surrounding earth.

Drainage Systems:

A well-designed **drainage system** is critical for keeping the home dry. French drains, which are trenches filled with gravel and a perforated pipe, help channel water away from the foundation. In areas with heavy rainfall, **sloped landscaping** or **berms** can prevent water from pooling near the home. For homes on hillsides, terraces and retaining walls can be used to control water flow and reduce erosion.

Ventilation for Moisture Control:

In wet climates, good ventilation is necessary to prevent excess humidity inside the home. Without proper airflow, moisture can build up, leading to condensation and mold growth. **Dehumidifiers**, along with **ventilation systems** that bring in fresh air and expel moisture-laden air, are essential for keeping the home dry and comfortable.

4. Creating Homes That Are Storm- and Flood-Resistant

Earth-covered homes are naturally resilient to many types of extreme weather, but in regions prone to **storms** and **flooding**, additional precautions are necessary to ensure the safety and longevity of the home.

Storm Resistance:

Earth-covered homes are already well-suited to withstand **high winds** and **tornadoes** due to their low profile and the protective layer of earth surrounding the structure. However, in areas that experience hurricanes or other severe storms, additional reinforcement may be required. Reinforced **concrete walls** and **roof structures** can provide extra protection against flying debris and extreme pressure.

In coastal areas, where hurricanes are common, homes should be designed with **wind-resistant materials** and **storm shutters** to protect windows. The natural shape of earth-covered homes—often with rounded edges and low heights—reduces the impact of wind forces, making them more resilient than traditional homes during extreme weather events.

Flood Resistance:

Flooding can be a major concern in coastal or low-lying areas, but earth-covered homes can be designed to resist flooding by elevating the structure above expected flood levels or by incorporating **flood-resistant materials**. For homes in flood-prone areas, it's important to build on higher ground or use **stilts** to lift the home above floodwaters.

Proper drainage is essential to prevent water from pooling around the home during heavy rains. **Permeable surfaces** around the home can allow water to filter through the ground rather than accumulating on the surface. Additionally, installing **flood barriers** or designing **landscaping features** that direct water away from the home can reduce the risk of water damage.

Example: An Earth-Covered Home That Withstood a Hurricane Due to Smart Site Selection

In 2017, a family in the Gulf Coast region had their earth-covered home tested by the full force of a Category 4 hurricane. While many nearby homes suffered significant damage from high winds and flooding, their home emerged with only minor cosmetic damage.

The key to their home's resilience was **smart site selection**. Built into a gently sloping hillside, the home's design allowed water to naturally drain away, preventing any flooding. The home's **rounded edges** and earth-covered exterior protected it from wind damage, while the reinforced concrete walls and roof provided additional structural strength.

By positioning their home on elevated ground, away from low-lying flood-prone areas, and incorporating storm-resistant design features, the family's earth-covered home was able to withstand the hurricane with minimal impact. Their experience serves as a powerful example of how thoughtful planning and design can make an earth-covered home highly resilient in extreme weather conditions.

Conclusion: Climate-specific design is essential when building an earth-covered home, especially in regions with extreme weather conditions. Whether you're dealing with desert heat, coastal winds, or snowy winters, your home can be designed to not only survive but thrive. By focusing on natural light, ventilation, moisture control, and storm resistance, you can create a home that is both comfortable and durable, no matter the climate.

Once you've chosen the right site and adapted your design to the local climate, the next critical step is mastering construction techniques. Let's explore the unique building methods that will bring your earth-covered home to life.

7

Building Techniques for Earth-Covered Homes

eet **James**, an eco-conscious builder who has been working in sustainable construction for decades. In the early years of his career, James was deeply passionate about using traditional techniques like rammed earth and cob to create earth-covered homes. But over time, he saw the limitations of these methods, especially when it came to durability and scalability. Determined to make earth-covered homes more accessible and resilient, he began experimenting with modern construction techniques, like shotcrete and precast concrete panels, and incorporating recycled materials into his designs. His innovative approach not only improved the durability of his homes but also made them more affordable and easier to build. Today, James is a pioneer in the world of earth-covered construction, known for merging the best of traditional craftsmanship with cutting-edge technology.

Let's explore the techniques James and other builders use to create earth-covered homes, from time-honored methods to modern innovations, and how they can help you build a home that is both durable and sustainable.

Traditional vs. Modern Construction Techniques

The beauty of earth-covered homes lies in their ability to combine ancient building techniques with modern technology. While traditional methods like rammed earth, cob, and adobe have been used for centuries to build sturdy, sustainable homes, modern techniques offer new possibilities for improving durability, efficiency, and speed. In this section, we'll compare traditional and modern construction techniques, explore their advantages and drawbacks, and examine how recycled materials can be incorporated into innovative earth-covered designs.

1. Traditional Building Techniques: Rammed Earth, Cob, and Adobe

Rammed Earth

Rammed earth is one of the oldest and most durable building methods, dating back thousands of years. It involves compressing a mixture of earth, sand, and sometimes cement into forms to create solid, thick walls. The resulting structure is incredibly strong and has excellent thermal mass, which helps regulate indoor temperatures by absorbing and releasing heat.

Pros:

- Highly sustainable, using natural materials.
- Great thermal mass for energy efficiency.
- Long-lasting and durable with minimal maintenance.

Cons:

- Labor-intensive and time-consuming to build.
- Requires precise moisture content and careful compaction.
- Can be prone to cracking if not properly maintained.

Cob

Cob is another ancient technique that uses a mixture of clay, sand, straw, and water to create thick, sturdy walls. Cob homes are typically hand-sculpted, giving them a unique, organic look. The material is breathable and provides natural insulation, making it suitable for mild climates.

Pros:

- Simple and inexpensive materials.
- Flexible and sculptable, allowing for creative designs.
- Excellent thermal mass for stable indoor temperatures.

Cons:

- Requires constant maintenance to protect against moisture and erosion.

- Not suitable for regions with heavy rainfall or extreme cold.
- Building with cob can be labor-intensive and slow.

Adobe

Adobe is a traditional building method that involves forming bricks from a mixture of clay, sand, water, and straw, which are then dried in the sun. These bricks are stacked to form walls and are often coated with plaster for additional protection. Like rammed earth and cob, adobe has been used for centuries and offers excellent thermal properties.

Pros:

- Readily available and inexpensive materials.
- Energy-efficient with good thermal mass.
- Strong and durable when properly maintained.

Cons:

- Vulnerable to water damage if not properly sealed.
- Requires time for bricks to dry, slowing down construction.
- Not ideal for areas with high humidity or frequent rain.

2. Modern Techniques: Shotcrete and Precast Concrete Panels

Shotcrete

Shotcrete is a modern construction technique in which concrete is sprayed onto a surface at high velocity. This method is particularly useful for building earth-covered homes because it allows for seamless, curved surfaces that can be easily reinforced with steel. Shotcrete is often used to create **concrete domes** or structural walls that are later covered with earth.

Pros:

- Fast and efficient construction process.
- Strong and durable, with excellent resistance to moisture and weathering.
- Ideal for creating curved or dome-shaped structures.

Cons:

- More expensive than traditional methods due to the need for specialized equipment.
- Requires skilled labor for proper application.
- Less sustainable than natural materials like rammed earth or cob.

Precast Concrete Panels

Precast concrete panels are factory-made concrete sections that are transported to the construction site and assembled to form the walls or roof of a home. This method offers precision and speed, as the panels can be produced in a controlled environment and installed quickly on-site. Precast panels are often reinforced with steel for additional strength.

Pros:

- Faster construction compared to traditional methods.
- High precision and quality control in a factory setting.
- Durable, low-maintenance, and resistant to moisture and weather.

Cons:

- Higher initial cost compared to traditional materials.
- Requires heavy machinery for transportation and installation.
- May not blend as seamlessly with natural surroundings as traditional materials.

3. Incorporating Recycled Materials for Innovative Designs

One of the most exciting developments in earth-covered home construction is the use of **recycled materials**. By incorporating items like old tires, glass bottles, and reclaimed steel, builders can reduce waste, lower costs, and create homes with a smaller environmental footprint.

Tires (Earthships)

In some earth-covered homes, especially **Earthships**, used tires are filled with compacted earth and stacked to form walls. The tires provide excellent insulation and thermal mass, making them a perfect fit for earth-covered construction. Once the tire walls are covered with plaster or adobe, they are hidden from view, giving the home a smooth, natural look.

Pros:

- Reuses materials that would otherwise end up in landfills.
- Provides excellent insulation and thermal mass.
- Cost-effective and durable.

Cons:

- Tires are not biodegradable and may raise environmental concerns.
- Labor-intensive to fill and stack.
- Requires additional finishes to cover and seal the tires.

Recycled Glass and Steel

Recycled glass and steel can also be used creatively in earth-covered homes. For example, **glass bottles** can be embedded into walls to create beautiful, light-filtering designs, while reclaimed steel can be used for structural supports or decorative elements.

Pros:

- Reduces waste and promotes sustainability.
- Adds unique, artistic elements to the design.
- Strong and durable materials that enhance the structure's longevity.

Cons:

- Requires careful design to ensure structural integrity.
- Incorporating these materials can increase labor costs.
- May need additional insulation if not used properly.

4. Pros and Cons of Various Structural Supports (Concrete Domes, Wood Framing)

Earth-covered homes require strong structural support to withstand the weight of the earth above and around them. The choice of **structural support** depends on the design, materials, and local climate.

Concrete Domes

Concrete domes are a popular choice for earth-covered homes because they are incredibly strong and can support the weight of the earth without additional reinforcements. These structures are typically created using shotcrete and steel rebar and offer a high level of resistance to earthquakes, storms, and other natural disasters.

Pros:

- Extremely durable and low-maintenance.
- Can support significant loads without the need for internal columns.
- Ideal for curved or dome-shaped designs.

Cons:

- More expensive than other structural options.
- Requires specialized knowledge and equipment to build.
- Difficult to modify once built.

Wood Framing

Wood framing is another option for earth-covered homes, particularly in designs that incorporate **berms** or partial earth coverage rather than full underground construction. Wood is a renewable resource and provides flexibility in design, but it requires careful attention to moisture control.

Pros:

- Renewable and environmentally friendly material.
- Easy to work with and modify.
- Lower cost compared to concrete.

Cons:

- Vulnerable to moisture, rot, and pests if not properly sealed.
- Less durable than concrete for fully underground homes.
- Requires regular maintenance to ensure longevity.

Story: A Builder's Journey from Traditional to Modern Meth-

ods

For years, **Liam**, a builder specializing in sustainable homes, used traditional techniques like rammed earth and cob to create rustic, beautiful earth-covered homes. While his clients loved the aesthetic and eco-friendliness of these methods, Liam began to encounter issues with long-term durability, particularly in regions with harsh weather conditions. Cracks in the walls, moisture problems, and time-consuming construction processes were becoming recurring challenges.

Determined to improve the quality of his homes, Liam started exploring modern construction methods. He began experimenting with **shotcrete**, creating durable concrete domes that could withstand heavy rain, wind, and even earthquakes. He also incorporated **precast concrete panels** for faster, more precise construction. In addition, Liam began using recycled materials like old tires and glass to enhance the sustainability and uniqueness of his designs.

The transition wasn't easy—there was a learning curve, and some of the techniques required new equipment and skills. But over time, Liam saw the benefits. His homes became more resilient, required less maintenance, and could be built more quickly and affordably. Today, Liam's earth-covered homes are a blend of the old and the new, combining the beauty of traditional methods with the strength and efficiency of modern technology.

Conclusion: Building an earth-covered home offers a wide range of construction techniques, from time-honored methods like rammed earth and cob to modern innovations like shotcrete and precast concrete panels. Each approach has its advantages and drawbacks, but by understanding your options, you can choose the techniques that best suit your design, budget, and climate. Builders like Liam demonstrate that merging traditional craftsmanship with cutting-edge technology can result in homes that are not only more durable and sustainable but also quicker and more cost-effective to build.

Now that you've mastered the building techniques, it's time to think about energy systems. In the next chapter, we'll explore how to integrate renewable energy sources to create a self-sustaining, off-grid earth-covered home.

Waterproofing and Insulating an Earth-Covered Home

When building an earth-covered home, waterproofing and insulation are two of the most critical elements to get right. The unique structure of these homes—where much of the building is underground or surrounded by earth—means that moisture and temperature control are key to maintaining the longevity and comfort of the home. Without proper waterproofing and insulation, you risk structural damage, mold, and uncomfortable living conditions. In this chapter, we'll explore the best practices for keeping your earth-covered home dry, warm, and energy-efficient.

The Critical Importance of Waterproofing in Earth-Covered Homes

Waterproofing is absolutely essential in earth-covered homes because these structures are constantly exposed to moisture from the surrounding soil. Without effective waterproofing, water can seep into the home's walls and foundation, leading to mold growth, structural damage, and unhealthy living conditions. The soil surrounding the home can retain moisture for long periods, so it's crucial that your home is fully sealed to prevent water infiltration.

Water damage can manifest in several ways, including:

- **Foundation cracks** caused by water pressure from satu-rated soil.
- **Mold and mildew** growth in damp, poorly ventilated spaces.
- **Wall and floor degradation**, as moisture can weaken materials over time.

To prevent these issues, it's critical to incorporate multiple layers of waterproofing into the design of your earth-covered home. Each layer plays a specific role in keeping moisture out and ensuring the longevity of the structure.

Best Practices for Exterior Membrane Systems, Drainage Layers, and Insulation

There are several key components to creating a waterproof, insulated earth-covered home. These include **exterior membrane systems**, **drainage layers**, and **thermal insulation**. When these elements are properly integrated, they work together to protect the home from moisture and temperature extremes.

Exterior Membrane Systems

The first line of defense against water infiltration is the **waterproof membrane** applied to the exterior of the home. This membrane is typically a flexible, durable material that covers the home's foundation and walls, creating a continuous barrier to prevent water from entering.

Types of waterproof membranes:

- **Bituminous Membranes**: Made from asphalt or bitumen, these are widely used for their durability and flexibility. They can be applied as a liquid or as sheets, providing a seamless layer of protection.
- **EPDM (Ethylene Propylene Diene Monomer)**: A synthetic rubber material that is highly resistant to weathering, UV light, and water. EPDM membranes are commonly used in green roof applications due to their flexibility and durability.
- **Bentonite Clay Panels**: These panels expand when exposed to water, forming a watertight seal around the home.

Bentonite is often used in high-moisture environments or where groundwater pressure is a concern.

Drainage Layers

In addition to the membrane, **drainage layers** are essential for directing water away from the home. Even the best waterproof membrane won't last long if water is allowed to accumulate around the structure. Drainage layers are typically placed between the membrane and the surrounding soil, ensuring that any water that reaches the home is quickly diverted away.

Best practices for drainage:

- **French Drains**: These are trenches filled with gravel and a perforated pipe that collects and redirects water away from the home's foundation.
- **Gravel or Aggregate Drainage**: A layer of gravel or small stones can be placed around the home to allow water to drain through the soil and into a designated drainage system.
- **Drainage Panels**: These panels are installed between the waterproof membrane and the soil, allowing water to flow freely down the wall and into the drainage system.

Proper drainage is especially important for homes built on hillsides, where rainwater can accumulate at the base of the slope. By installing a well-designed drainage system, you reduce the pressure on your waterproofing membrane and minimize the risk of leaks or water damage.

Insulation

In an earth-covered home, **insulation** serves two key purposes: it helps maintain a stable indoor temperature and protects the waterproof membrane from temperature fluctuations. The insulating layer is usually installed over the waterproof membrane to keep the home warm in winter and cool in summer.

Types of insulation for earth-covered homes:

- **Extruded Polystyrene (XPS)**: This rigid foam insulation is commonly used in earth-covered homes due to its high resistance to moisture and its ability to retain its insulating properties over time.
- **Spray Foam Insulation**: While more expensive, spray foam provides an excellent thermal barrier and can be applied in irregular spaces to create an airtight seal.
- **Rockwool**: Made from volcanic rock, rockwool insulation is resistant to fire, water, and pests, making it a durable option for earth-covered homes.

The insulation layer is crucial for energy efficiency, ensuring that the thermal mass of the surrounding earth doesn't lead to unwanted heat gain or loss.

Green Roofs and Their Role in Insulation and Waterproofing

Green roofs are an integral part of many earth-covered homes. They not only enhance the home's ability to blend into the landscape but also provide additional insulation and waterproofing.

How Green Roofs Work

A green roof consists of several layers, including a waterproof membrane, a root barrier, a drainage layer, and a layer of soil or growing medium. Together, these layers help to absorb and redirect rainwater, preventing it from reaching the home's structure. The soil and vegetation also provide natural insulation, reducing heat transfer through the roof.

Benefits of green roofs:

- **Improved insulation**: The soil and plants on a green roof act as a natural insulator, keeping the home cooler in summer and warmer in winter. This reduces the need for artificial heating and cooling, saving energy and lowering utility bills.
- **Stormwater management**: Green roofs absorb rainwater, reducing the amount of runoff that can cause flooding or erosion around the home. The water that is absorbed by the plants and soil is slowly released back into the atmosphere through evaporation, reducing the burden on drainage systems.
- **Increased lifespan of waterproofing materials**: By covering the waterproof membrane with a layer of soil and plants, green roofs protect it from UV radiation, temperature fluctuations, and physical damage. This extends the lifespan of the membrane and reduces the need for repairs or replacements.

While green roofs offer many benefits, it's important to ensure that they are properly installed and maintained. The waterproof membrane beneath the roof must be strong enough to handle the weight of the soil and plants, and the drainage system needs to be effective in preventing water buildup.

Managing Condensation and Humidity Inside the Home

While waterproofing focuses on keeping external water out of the home, managing **condensation** and **humidity** inside the home is equally important. Earth-covered homes can be more prone to moisture buildup due to their enclosed, insulated structure, so proper ventilation and moisture control measures are essential.

Ventilation:

A well-designed **ventilation system** ensures that moisture-laden air doesn't become trapped inside the home. In humid climates, cross-ventilation through operable windows or mechanical ventilation systems can help keep the air fresh and dry. Additionally, dehumidifiers can be used in problem areas like bathrooms and kitchens.

Condensation Control:

Condensation often occurs when warm, moist air comes into contact with cooler surfaces, like walls or windows. To prevent condensation, it's important to use vapor barriers and insulation that keep the interior surfaces warm enough to avoid water droplets forming.

In particularly humid regions, using materials that absorb

and release moisture, such as **clay plaster** or **bamboo**, can help regulate indoor humidity levels. These materials breathe, allowing moisture to escape rather than accumulating in the walls.

Case Study: A Homeowner's Struggle with Moisture Issues and How They Resolved It

David and **Sarah** were excited about building their dream earth-covered home in a humid, coastal region. However, a few months after moving in, they noticed signs of moisture problems: musty smells, condensation on the windows, and small patches of mold in the corners of some rooms.

They soon realized that the drainage system around their home wasn't adequate to handle the high levels of rainfall in their area. Water was pooling around the foundation, and the home's interior ventilation wasn't strong enough to prevent moisture buildup.

To resolve the issue, they worked with a contractor to install **French drains** and improve the slope of the land around the home, directing water away from the foundation. They also upgraded their ventilation system to include a **heat recovery ventilator (HRV)**, which exchanged humid indoor air for fresh, dry outdoor air without losing heat.

In addition, David and Sarah added a **vapor barrier** to the walls and replaced some of the home's insulation with a more moisture-resistant material. Within weeks, the musty smells disappeared, and their home became dry and comfortable again. This experience reinforced the importance of thorough waterproofing and ventilation in any earth-covered home.

Conclusion: Waterproofing and insulation are two of the most critical aspects of building a successful earth-covered home. From exterior membranes and drainage layers to green roofs and indoor humidity control, every detail must be carefully planned and executed to keep your home dry, energy-efficient, and comfortable. As David and Sarah's experience shows, addressing these issues early on can save you from costly problems down the road.

Now that you've mastered the essentials of waterproofing and insulation, it's time to explore the next frontier—energy systems. In the following chapter, we'll look at how to incorporate renewable energy into your earth-covered home for a self-sustaining, off-grid lifestyle

Ventilation and Natural Lighting Solutions

When designing an earth-covered home, ensuring proper **ventilation** and access to **natural light** is essential to creating a healthy, comfortable living space. Since these homes are often built partially or fully underground, they can face challenges in maintaining good airflow and bright interiors. However, with thoughtful design, it's possible to integrate solutions that bring in fresh air and natural light while maintaining the energy efficiency and sustainability of the home. In this chapter, we'll explore different strategies for ventilation and natural lighting in earth-covered homes, from solar tubes to courtyards, and highlight the importance of each in creating a livable environment.

The Importance of Proper Ventilation in Earth-Covered Homes

Proper **ventilation** is critical in earth-covered homes because their unique structure can limit the natural flow of air. Without adequate ventilation, these homes can become stuffy, accumulate humidity, or even trap harmful pollutants, leading to unhealthy indoor air quality. In traditional homes, windows and doors provide ample airflow, but earth-covered homes require special attention to how air moves through the space.

Good ventilation helps to:

- **Regulate indoor humidity** and prevent the buildup of moisture, which can lead to mold growth.
- **Reduce indoor air pollutants** like dust, pet dander, and chemicals from household products.
- Ensure **healthy oxygen levels** and remove excess carbon dioxide from indoor air.
- Maintain **consistent indoor temperatures** by promoting air circulation.

In earth-covered homes, a well-designed ventilation system can make all the difference. Relying solely on mechanical systems like HVAC is less energy-efficient, so incorporating natural ventilation techniques like cross-ventilation, combined with mechanical systems when needed, is the best approach for maintaining indoor air quality.

Solar Tubes, Skylights, and Strategically Placed Windows for Natural Light

One of the challenges of building a home partially or entirely underground is providing enough **natural light**. Sunlight is crucial not just for visibility but also for the psychological well-being of the occupants. A bright, naturally lit interior makes the home feel welcoming and reduces the need for artificial lighting, lowering energy consumption.

Here are some of the most effective ways to bring natural light into an earth-covered home:

1. Solar Tubes

Solar tubes, also known as **light tubes** or **sun tunnels**, are an innovative solution for bringing daylight into parts of the home that don't have direct access to windows. These tubes are installed through the roof or exterior walls, capturing sunlight and directing it into dark or windowless rooms via reflective tubing. Solar tubes are energy-efficient, cost-effective, and easy to install, making them a great option for earth-covered homes.

Advantages of solar tubes:

- They bring natural light to **basements or interior rooms** that lack windows.
- **Energy-efficient** as they reduce the need for artificial lighting during the day.
- Simple installation without major structural changes.

2. Skylights

Skylights are another excellent option for bringing light into earth-covered homes, particularly those with green roofs or limited wall space for windows. Skylights can be placed strategically in rooms that need more daylight and can also provide **ventilation** when operable. Modern skylights are designed with energy efficiency in mind, offering insulated glass to prevent heat loss in colder climates.

Benefits of skylights:

- They provide **direct natural light** to areas below ground level.
- Can be designed as **vented skylights** to improve airflow.
- They contribute to **passive solar heating** in colder climates by allowing sunlight to warm the interior.

3. Strategically Placed Windows

While windows are a standard feature in any home, their placement in an earth-covered home is particularly important. Since many of the walls are built into the earth, the **exposed sides** of the home should have large, well-placed windows to maximize daylight. South-facing windows are ideal for capturing sunlight throughout the day, while east- and west-facing windows bring in morning and evening light.

Key strategies for window placement:

- Place large windows on **south-facing walls** to maximize passive solar gain.
- Use **clerestory windows** (high windows placed near the

roofline) to bring in light while maintaining privacy and reducing glare.
- Design **light wells**—openings in the earth surrounding the home that allow light to enter from above—especially in homes with extensive earth-berming.

Ventilation Systems to Ensure Healthy Indoor Air Quality

Given the challenges of airflow in earth-covered homes, it's often necessary to install a **mechanical ventilation system** to complement natural ventilation techniques. The goal is to ensure that fresh air circulates throughout the home while removing stale, humid, or polluted air.

1. Heat Recovery Ventilators (HRVs) and Energy Recovery Ventilators (ERVs)

HRVs and **ERVs** are mechanical systems that exchange stale indoor air with fresh outdoor air while recovering heat (or in the case of ERVs, heat and humidity). These systems are highly energy-efficient because they reduce the amount of heat lost when ventilating the home in the winter, or they minimize heat gain in the summer. HRVs and ERVs are ideal for tightly sealed homes like earth-covered houses, where natural ventilation alone may not be sufficient.

Benefits of HRVs and ERVs:

- Provide **continuous fresh air** without sacrificing energy efficiency.
- Help maintain **indoor humidity levels**, particularly in humid climates.
- Improve **air quality** by filtering incoming air.

2. Cross-Ventilation

Cross-ventilation occurs when air enters the home from one side and exits from another, creating a natural breeze through the space. This can be achieved by placing **operable windows** or **vents** on opposite walls, allowing fresh air to flow through the home. Earth-covered homes can incorporate cross-ventilation by designing rooms that have access to at least two exterior walls or by creating air channels that direct airflow throughout the home.

Cross-ventilation considerations:

- Best suited for homes with **multiple exterior exposures**, such as hillside homes or homes with courtyards.
- **Operable skylights** can help enhance cross-ventilation by releasing hot air from the top of the home.

3. Earth Tubes

Earth tubes are an innovative ventilation system that uses the natural temperature of the earth to pre-cool or pre-heat incoming air. These underground tubes draw air from outside, passing it through the earth before entering the home. Because the earth's temperature remains relatively constant year-round, the air that flows through the tubes is naturally cooler in summer and warmer in winter, reducing the need for additional heating or cooling.

Advantages of earth tubes:

- They provide **natural temperature regulation** without the need for energy-intensive systems.
- Can be used in combination with other ventilation methods for a more comprehensive system.

Designing Courtyards and Atriums to Bring in Light and Air

Courtyards and atriums are architectural features that can bring significant amounts of natural light and fresh air into earth-covered homes, particularly in homes that have large portions built underground. These spaces act as **light wells** and **air channels**, providing ventilation and creating bright, open areas in the heart of the home.

1. Central Courtyards

A **central courtyard** is an open-air space located in the middle of the home, surrounded by interior walls. This design allows light and air to reach the rooms that may otherwise be dark or poorly ventilated. In earth-covered homes, courtyards can be particularly effective for homes built into hillsides or berms, where the exterior walls may not have direct access to sunlight.

Benefits of central courtyards:

- They bring **natural light** deep into the home, reducing the need for artificial lighting.
- Act as **ventilation shafts**, allowing hot air to rise and escape while pulling in cooler air from lower levels.
- Create an **outdoor living space** that is protected from the elements and surrounded by the home's structure.

2. Atriums

An **atrium** is similar to a courtyard but is typically enclosed by a glass roof or walls. Atriums can function as interior green spaces or light wells, providing daylight and ventilation to interior rooms that don't have access to exterior windows.

Advantages of atriums:

- Provide **year-round natural light** even in colder climates where fully open courtyards may not be practical.
- Can be used as **indoor gardens**, improving air quality and creating a connection to nature.
- Serve as **central hubs** for passive ventilation, especially when combined with operable skylights or vents.

Example: A Home with a Central Courtyard Acting as a Light Well

A stunning example of how courtyards can transform earth-covered homes is the **Hawthorne Residence**—a modern, earth-bermed home built into a hillside. The designers of this home incorporated a **central courtyard** that acts as a light well, bringing daylight and fresh air into the home's interior spaces. The courtyard is open to the sky, providing natural light to every room that surrounds it, while also allowing air to circulate freely throughout the house.

In addition to bringing in light, the courtyard serves as an **outdoor gathering space** that the homeowners use year-round. The walls of the courtyard are lined with floor-to-ceiling windows, ensuring that even the deepest parts of the home remain bright and airy. On hot days, the open design of the courtyard creates natural cross-ventilation, pulling cool air into the home and releasing warm air through operable skylights.

The Hawthorne Residence demonstrates how smart design can overcome the challenges of building an earth-covered home, providing both light and air in a structure that is largely underground.

Conclusion: Proper ventilation and natural lighting are essential to making an earth-covered home comfortable and healthy. From solar tubes and skylights to central courtyards and innovative ventilation systems, there are numerous strategies to ensure your home feels bright and fresh, even if it's surrounded by earth. By incorporating these solutions into your design, you can create a space that feels open, airy, and connected to the natural world.

Now that you understand the construction and design techniques needed to bring your earth-covered home to life, let's explore the financial side of the process—how to budget, finance, and plan for your eco-friendly dream home

8

Budgeting and Financing

While it's true that building an earth-covered home might require a larger initial investment compared to a traditional home, the long-term benefits often outweigh the upfront costs. Here's a shocking fact: Earth-covered homes can **pay for themselves** in as little as **10 years** through energy savings alone. But to truly understand how these homes fit into your financial plans, you'll need to break down the costs, consider long-term savings, and explore financing options that can help you make your eco-friendly dream home a reality.

Breaking Down the Costs

Before diving into the financial benefits of earth-covered homes, it's important to understand how the **upfront costs** differ from those of traditional homes. While some aspects of building an earth-covered home are more expensive, others can help balance or even reduce costs over time. Let's break down the different factors that influence the budget for an earth-covered home, including excavation, materials, and labor, and explore the long-term savings these homes provide.

1. Comparing the Costs of Earth-Covered Homes vs. Traditional Homes

When comparing the costs of earth-covered homes to traditional homes, the upfront investment can sometimes be higher. This is mainly due to the unique **site preparation**, specialized **materials**, and **construction techniques** required for earth-covered structures. Here's a closer look at the key differences:

Earth-Covered Homes:

- **Excavation**: One of the most significant cost drivers for earth-covered homes is the excavation needed to either partially bury the structure or create berms around it. Excavation costs vary depending on the site's topography, soil type, and the depth of the build. However, a well-chosen site can minimize excavation costs, especially if you're building into a hillside.
- **Specialized Materials**: Earth-covered homes often use materials that are more durable and energy-efficient than those in traditional homes, such as reinforced concrete, waterproof membranes, and high-quality insulation. These materials may cost more upfront, but they offer long-term savings by reducing energy consumption and maintenance.

- **Labor and Expertise**: Builders with experience in earth-covered construction may charge more due to the specialized techniques involved. However, this expertise ensures a longer-lasting, more resilient structure, which can save money over time.

Traditional Homes:

- **Standard Construction Materials**: Traditional homes are generally built with wood framing, which is cheaper upfront but may require more frequent maintenance and repairs, particularly in regions prone to pests, mold, or extreme weather.
- **Roofing and Siding Costs**: Traditional homes require roofing and siding that must be replaced or maintained regularly, adding to the long-term costs of ownership.
- **Utilities and HVAC**: Traditional homes often rely on more energy-intensive HVAC systems due to poor insulation and higher exposure to the elements, which drives up energy bills.

2. The Role of Excavation, Materials, and Labor in Cost Determination

The three major cost categories in any earth-covered home project are **excavation**, **materials**, and **labor**. Understanding how these factors impact the overall budget can help you plan more effectively.

Excavation Costs

Excavation is one of the biggest expenses in earth-covered home construction, especially if the site requires significant modification. The cost of excavation can vary widely depending on the site conditions:

- **Hillsides**: If you build into a naturally sloping site, excavation costs can be lower because the terrain already offers the depth and earth cover needed for the home.
- **Flat Land**: Building on flat land often requires creating berms or digging down to cover the home, which can increase excavation costs.

Material Costs

The materials used in earth-covered homes are generally chosen for their durability, insulating properties, and resistance to moisture. While these materials may cost more initially, they offer significant long-term savings:

- **Reinforced Concrete**: Used for structural support, concrete is highly durable but more expensive than wood framing.
- **Waterproof Membranes**: Essential for protecting the home from moisture, these membranes are a non-negotiable expense but help prevent costly repairs in the future.
- **Insulation**: High-quality insulation, such as extruded polystyrene (XPS) or spray foam, is key to maintaining a stable indoor temperature, reducing the need for heating

and cooling.

Labor Costs

Experienced builders who specialize in earth-covered construction often charge more due to the complexity of the project. However, this investment in skilled labor can pay off by ensuring that the home is built correctly the first time, minimizing future maintenance and repair costs.

3. Ongoing Savings from Energy Efficiency and Low Maintenance

One of the biggest financial advantages of an earth-covered home is the **ongoing savings** it offers, particularly in terms of energy efficiency and low maintenance requirements. While traditional homes are exposed to the elements, requiring regular repairs and high energy use for heating and cooling, earth-covered homes offer significant cost reductions over time.

Energy Efficiency

Earth-covered homes are naturally insulated by the surrounding soil, which helps regulate indoor temperatures year-round. The thermal mass of the earth stabilizes the temperature, keeping the home cool in the summer and warm in the winter. This means you'll rely far less on HVAC systems, leading to lower energy bills.

- **Heating and Cooling Savings**: On average, earth-covered homes can reduce energy use by **60-80%** compared to traditional homes.
- **Passive Solar Heating**: When designed with large, south-facing windows, earth-covered homes can use **passive solar heating** to further reduce energy costs in colder climates.

Low Maintenance

Because much of the structure is buried in the earth, earth-covered homes are protected from many of the maintenance issues that plague traditional homes, such as roof replacements, siding repairs, and pest control. Here's how these homes save on maintenance:

- **Roofing and Siding**: Green roofs or earth-covered roofs require little to no maintenance compared to traditional roofing materials, which need replacement every 20-30 years.
- **Pest Resistance**: Earth-covered homes are less susceptible to termite infestations, rot, and mold, especially when built with concrete and other durable materials.

4. Long-Term Cost Projections for Utilities and Upkeep

The real financial advantage of an earth-covered home comes into play over the long term. While you might spend more upfront on excavation, materials, and labor, the ongoing savings from reduced utility bills and lower maintenance costs can add up significantly over time. Let's look at some projected cost savings over the life of the home:

Energy Savings

Traditional homes typically have higher energy costs due to their exposure to the elements. In contrast, an earth-covered home's natural insulation can cut heating and cooling expenses dramatically. Over 10 years, a typical earth-covered home might save:

- **$15,000-$30,000** in heating and cooling costs, depending on climate and energy prices.

Maintenance Savings

Earth-covered homes require less frequent maintenance, thanks to their durable materials and protection from the elements. Over 20 years, you could save:

- **$10,000-$20,000** on roofing, siding, and exterior repairs compared to a traditional home.

Example: A Financial Breakdown of Two Similar-Sized Homes (Earth-Covered vs. Traditional)

Let's take a look at an example comparing two homes of similar size—one earth-covered and one traditional. For this example, we'll consider a **2,000-square-foot** home in a temperate climate:

Expense Category
Earth-Covered Home vs
Traditional Home

Initial Build Cost

$300,000

$250,000

Excavation

$15,000

$5,000

Materials (concrete, insulation, waterproofing)

$90,000

$60,000

Energy Costs (10 years)

$12,000

$40,000

Maintenance (20 years)

$5,000

$20,000

Total 20-Year Cost

$332,000

$355,000

While the earth-covered home has higher upfront costs due to excavation and specialized materials, the **total cost over 20 years** is lower because of reduced energy consumption and maintenance.

Conclusion: Building an earth-covered home requires careful financial planning, but the long-term savings in energy and maintenance make it a smart investment. While the initial costs may be higher, the benefits of energy efficiency and low maintenance often outweigh these expenses over time, leading to significant savings in the long run.

Now that we've covered the financial side, it's time to dive into the exciting world of renewable energy integration. In the next chapter, we'll explore how to make your earth-covered home even more sustainable by incorporating solar, wind, and geothermal systems for off-grid living

Financing and Incentives for Earth-Covered Homes

Building an earth-covered home is an exciting venture, but financing such a project can seem challenging due to its non-traditional nature. Fortunately, there are numerous **financing options**, **government incentives**, and **green building grants** that can help make your dream home more affordable. From energy-efficient loans to tax incentives for sustainable construction, there are many resources available to assist you in financing your earth-covered home.

In this chapter, we'll explore various ways to fund your project, including the types of loans available for eco-friendly homes, government grants and tax incentives, and how you can tap into support from green building organizations.

Financing Options for Alternative Home Construction

Financing an earth-covered home can be a little more complicated than securing a traditional mortgage, but there are plenty of **loan options** specifically designed for alternative construction projects, including eco-friendly homes. Some lenders specialize in green construction, offering loans that take into account the long-term benefits of energy efficiency, while others may require a bit more effort to find. Here are some of the most common financing options for earth-covered homes.

1. Construction Loans

Since earth-covered homes are considered non-traditional builds, you may need to start with a **construction loan**. Construction loans are short-term loans that provide the necessary funding for building the home. Once construction is complete, these loans are often converted into permanent mortgages.

What to Expect:

- **Down payment**: Construction loans often require a larger down payment—typically around **20-25%** of the project cost—due to the additional risks involved in non-traditional construction.
- **Detailed building plans**: Lenders will want to see a detailed **construction plan** and budget, including information about your contractor and materials, to ensure that the project is feasible.
- **Conversion to mortgage**: After construction is finished,

the loan is typically converted into a permanent mortgage, which can be either a traditional or energy-efficient mortgage.

2. Energy-Efficient Mortgages (EEMs)

Energy-Efficient Mortgages (EEMs) are designed to help homeowners finance energy-efficient homes or make energy-saving improvements. These loans are ideal for earth-covered homes, which typically have lower energy demands due to their natural insulation and passive solar designs. EEMs allow lenders to extend the amount of the loan based on the energy savings that will result from the home's efficiency.

Advantages of EEMs:

- **Higher loan limits**: Lenders may offer larger loan amounts because the energy savings will lower your overall expenses.
- **Easier qualification**: The reduced energy bills associated with earth-covered homes make it easier to qualify for these loans, even if the upfront cost of construction is higher.
- **Lower long-term costs**: By locking in financing for energy-efficient upgrades, you can reduce your utility costs significantly, which offsets the initial expense.

3. Personal Loans and Green Lending Programs

If you're having trouble securing a construction loan or mortgage for your earth-covered home, another option is a **per-**

sonal loan or a **green lending program**. Some financial institutions and organizations offer loans specifically for eco-friendly projects.

Green lending programs often have favorable terms for home-owners pursuing sustainable construction, such as lower interest rates or more flexible repayment options. These loans can be a great way to fill gaps in financing or cover specific eco-friendly aspects of your home, such as renewable energy systems or green roofs.

Government Grants and Tax Incentives for Eco-Friendly Buildings

One of the most significant advantages of building an earth-covered home is that you may qualify for a variety of **government grants** and **tax incentives** aimed at encouraging sustainable construction. These programs are designed to offset the higher initial costs of green building practices, making eco-friendly homes more accessible to a broader range of homeowners.

1. Federal Tax Incentives

The U.S. government offers several **tax credits** and **deductions** for homeowners who invest in energy-efficient homes. These incentives can substantially reduce the cost of building an earth-covered home, especially if your design includes renewable energy systems, like solar panels or geothermal heating.

- **Residential Energy Efficient Property Credit**: This federal tax credit covers up to **30%** of the cost of installing renewable energy systems, such as solar panels, wind turbines, or geothermal systems. Since earth-covered homes often pair well with renewable energy, this credit can help offset installation costs.
- **Energy Star Home Tax Credit**: If your earth-covered home meets **Energy Star** requirements for energy efficiency, you could qualify for this tax credit, which provides up to **$2,000** for new homes that exceed certain energy standards.

2. State and Local Grants

In addition to federal programs, many **states** and **local governments** offer grants or tax incentives for sustainable home construction. These programs vary widely depending on where you live, but some states offer direct grants for building energy-efficient homes, while others provide property tax reductions for homes with energy-saving features.

For example:

- **California Solar Initiative**: This program provides incentives for homeowners who install solar systems, reducing upfront costs by offering rebates based on the size of the system and the amount of energy saved.
- **New York State Energy Research and Development Authority (NYSERDA)**: Offers incentives for homes that meet energy-efficiency criteria through the **New York Home Performance with Energy Star** program.

3. Property-Assessed Clean Energy (PACE) Programs

PACE programs allow homeowners to finance energy-efficient improvements through a special assessment added to their property tax bill. While PACE loans are typically used for renewable energy installations or energy-efficient upgrades, they can be a valuable resource for financing earth-covered homes that already incorporate many of these elements.

Benefits of PACE financing:

- **No upfront costs**: You can finance the improvements with no money down, making it easier to invest in expensive green technologies like solar panels or high-efficiency windows.
- **Repayment through property taxes**: The loan is repaid as part of your property tax bill, making it easier to manage financially.

Understanding Loans for Energy-Efficient Homes

When you're planning to build an earth-covered home, it's essential to explore loans designed specifically for **energy-efficient homes**. These loans take into account the long-term savings generated by the home's reduced energy consumption, allowing you to borrow more money upfront for construction while keeping your overall costs manageable.

1. Fannie Mae's HomeStyle Energy Mortgage

Fannie Mae offers the **HomeStyle Energy Mortgage**, which allows borrowers to finance energy-efficient upgrades as part of their mortgage. This loan can be particularly helpful for homeowners building earth-covered homes, as it allows for the inclusion of **energy-saving technologies** such as insulation, solar panels, and energy-efficient windows.

How it works:

- You can borrow up to **15% of the home's appraised value** for energy-saving improvements.
- Energy upgrades must be documented through an **energy report** or **audit** showing the expected savings.
- This loan is ideal for earth-covered homes, which often require higher upfront investment but deliver long-term energy savings.

2. FHA 203(k) Loan

The **FHA 203(k) loan** is a renovation loan that allows you to finance both the purchase and improvement of a home. While it's typically used for fixer-uppers, this loan can also be applied to eco-friendly upgrades, such as installing renewable energy systems or improving the home's insulation.

Advantages of the FHA 203(k) loan:

- **Lower down payment requirements**: You can borrow up to **110% of the home's projected value** after improvements.

- Ideal for projects that need substantial work, such as energy retrofits or major eco-friendly renovations.

Securing Investment from Green Building Organizations

In addition to government incentives and loans, you may be able to secure **investment or grants** from organizations that support **green building initiatives**. Many non-profits, foundations, and private companies are committed to advancing sustainable construction and may offer financial assistance or grants to homeowners pursuing innovative eco-friendly projects.

1. LEED Certification Grants

If you're aiming for **LEED certification** (Leadership in Energy and Environmental Design) for your earth-covered home, you may be eligible for grants or financial incentives from green building organizations. LEED-certified homes must meet rigorous standards for sustainability, energy efficiency, and environmental impact, making them attractive to investors and grant programs focused on eco-friendly construction.

2. Green Building Funds

Organizations like the **Green Building Fund** or the **Sustainable Buildings Initiative** provide funding for projects that promote environmental sustainability. These funds may offer grants or low-interest loans to support energy-efficient designs, including earth-covered homes.

How to qualify:

- Your home must meet certain **sustainability criteria**, such as energy efficiency, water conservation, or use of renewable materials.
- You may need to submit a detailed **project proposal** outlining the environmental benefits of your home design.

Case Study: A Homeowner Who Financed Their Earth-Covered Home Using Sustainable Building Grants

Meet **Alex and Casey**, a couple who had always dreamed of building an eco-friendly home but were unsure how to finance their ambitious project. After researching various options, they discovered a combination of **sustainable building grants** and **energy-efficient mortgages** that helped them bring their earth-covered home to life.

They applied for the **Residential Energy Efficient Property Credit**, which covered 30% of the cost of their solar panel installation, and used a local **green building grant** to fund the installation of a geothermal heating and cooling system. Additionally, they qualified for a **HomeStyle Energy Mortgage** from Fannie Mae, which allowed them to borrow extra money to install high-quality insulation and energy-efficient windows.

By combining these financing options with their personal savings, Alex and Casey were able to build their earth-covered home within budget. Today, they enjoy lower utility bills, minimal maintenance costs, and the satisfaction of knowing they've made a positive environmental impact—all thanks to smart financing and sustainability-focused grants.

Conclusion: Financing an earth-covered home might seem daunting, but with the right combination of **loans**, **government incentives**, and **green building grants**, it can be a financially feasible project. By taking advantage of these resources, you can reduce your upfront costs, secure better financing terms, and enjoy long-term savings from energy-efficient design.

Now that we've covered the financial strategies for building an earth-covered home, it's time to explore how to integrate renewable energy systems to make your home truly sustainable and off-grid.

Return on Investment for Earth-Covered Homes

Building an earth-covered home is not just about creating a sustainable, energy-efficient space—it's also a long-term investment. Over time, these homes tend to increase in value, particularly as the demand for sustainable and resilient housing continues to grow. While earth-covered homes may have higher upfront costs, the combination of lower utility bills, minimal maintenance, and their appeal in the growing market for eco-conscious buyers makes them a financially sound decision.

In this chapter, we'll explore how earth-covered homes increase property value, the factors that influence resale potential, and why sustainable homes are becoming more attractive to buyers. We'll also look at the environmental and financial benefits over time, culminating in the story of a couple whose earth-covered home tripled in value over 15 years.

How Earth-Covered Homes Increase Property Value Over Time

One of the primary financial advantages of an earth-covered home is its ability to **appreciate in value** as sustainability and energy efficiency become more desirable in the real estate market. Several factors contribute to this increase in property value over time, including reduced operational costs, environmental benefits, and the growing market for green homes.

Energy Efficiency and Cost Savings

Earth-covered homes are known for their exceptional **energy efficiency**, which reduces the cost of heating, cooling, and general maintenance. Because these homes are naturally insulated by the surrounding earth, they consume far less energy than traditional homes. Over time, these savings not only reduce the owner's utility bills but also increase the home's appeal to future buyers, who may see long-term financial benefits in purchasing an energy-efficient home.

Durability and Low Maintenance

Unlike traditional homes, earth-covered homes are built with durable materials like reinforced concrete, steel, and thick insulation. These structures are also protected from the elements by the surrounding earth, making them less prone to weather-related wear and tear. This **low maintenance** advantage adds to the home's long-term value, as buyers are increasingly seeking properties that won't require frequent repairs or updates.

Appeal to Eco-Conscious Buyers

As more people become aware of the environmental impact of traditional homes, there's a growing market for **eco-friendly** and **resilient** housing. Earth-covered homes, with their minimal environmental footprint, appeal to a specific niche of buyers who prioritize sustainability. These homes are often seen as innovative and forward-thinking, which can boost their market value as interest in green building continues to rise.

Resale Considerations: How Buyers View Earth-Covered Homes

While earth-covered homes offer numerous benefits, it's important to understand how buyers perceive them. These homes can be incredibly attractive to the right market, but there are certain factors to consider when selling an earth-covered property.

Educating Buyers

Many potential buyers may not be familiar with the benefits of earth-covered homes. Educating buyers on the **energy savings**, **environmental advantages**, and **long-term durability** of the home is essential. Providing detailed information on the home's reduced energy consumption, low maintenance needs, and innovative design can help potential buyers see the value.

Unique Selling Points

Earth-covered homes often stand out in the market because of their unique architecture and eco-friendly design. Highlighting features like **green roofs**, **passive solar heating**, and **sustainable materials** can set the home apart from traditional properties. Additionally, emphasizing the resilience of the home against natural disasters—such as its ability to withstand wildfires, high winds, and even earthquakes—can appeal to buyers who prioritize safety and durability.

Niche Market Appeal

While the market for sustainable homes is growing, earth-covered homes may still appeal to a **niche market** of buyers who are particularly interested in green living or off-grid lifestyles. However, this niche is expanding as more people prioritize energy efficiency, sustainability, and resilience in their home purchases. As awareness of climate change and energy efficiency grows, this niche market is likely to become more mainstream.

The Growing Market for Sustainable and Resilient Homes

The real estate market is shifting, with an increasing number of buyers seeking **sustainable** and **resilient** homes that are designed to reduce environmental impact and withstand the effects of climate change. This shift presents an opportunity for earth-covered homes to become highly desirable properties.

Sustainability as a Selling Point

As sustainability becomes more important to homebuyers, **green homes** are gaining traction in the real estate market. According to studies, homes that are certified as energy-efficient or built with eco-friendly materials tend to sell faster and at higher prices than traditional homes. Earth-covered homes fit squarely within this trend, offering buyers an opportunity to live in a home that aligns with their environmental values.

Resilience in the Face of Climate Change

In addition to sustainability, **resilience** is a growing concern for homebuyers, particularly in regions prone to extreme weather events like hurricanes, wildfires, and flooding. Earth-covered homes are naturally resilient, as they are protected by the earth itself and built with materials that can withstand natural disasters. This resilience not only makes them more appealing to buyers but can also reduce insurance costs, adding further financial benefits.

Long-Term Market Growth

As governments and private institutions continue to push for more sustainable living, the demand for homes that meet environmental standards is likely to grow. Buyers are increasingly attracted to homes that promise lower carbon footprints, energy savings, and protection against the unpredictability of climate change. Earth-covered homes, which meet all of these criteria, are poised to see increasing demand in the coming years, leading to higher resale values.

Environmental and Financial Benefits in the Long Term

While the upfront cost of building an earth-covered home can be higher than a traditional home, the **long-term environmental and financial benefits** make it a wise investment.

Reduced Environmental Impact

Earth-covered homes are inherently more sustainable than traditional homes. They use fewer resources during construction, require less energy to operate, and have a much smaller carbon footprint over time. As climate change and environmental responsibility become more important, homes that prioritize sustainability are likely to see greater demand and increased property value.

Long-Term Financial Savings

The **energy savings** from an earth-covered home are substantial. Because these homes use natural insulation and passive solar design, they often have **significantly lower utility bills** than traditional homes. Over the course of decades, these savings can add up, making the overall cost of ownership much lower than a conventional house.

Additionally, because earth-covered homes require less maintenance and repairs due to their durable materials and protection from the elements, the **ongoing costs of upkeep** are also significantly reduced. This means that while you may pay more to build an earth-covered home, you'll spend less maintaining it, resulting in a higher return on investment.

Story: A Couple Who Saw Their Earth-Covered Home Triple in Value Over 15 Years

Janet and **Michael** were early adopters of sustainable living. In the early 2000s, they decided to build an earth-covered home in a rural area, motivated by their desire to reduce their environmental impact and live more efficiently. The initial cost was higher than they had expected—between the excavation, specialized materials, and renewable energy systems, the home cost about 30% more than a traditional house.

However, within a few years, they began to see the benefits. Their utility bills were incredibly low, thanks to the home's natural insulation and passive solar design. They rarely needed to turn on the air conditioning, and their heating bills were a fraction of what they had been in their previous home. Over time, the minimal maintenance costs became clear as well.

While their neighbors had to replace roofs, siding, and deal with pest issues, Janet and Michael's earth-covered home required little attention.

Fifteen years after building their home, Janet and Michael decided to move closer to their family. They were surprised to find that their home, which had been seen as unconventional when they first built it, had **tripled in value**. The real estate agent noted that the demand for eco-friendly, energy-efficient homes had skyrocketed in recent years, making their home highly desirable. What started as a personal passion project had turned into a significant financial gain.

Conclusion: Building an earth-covered home is not only an investment in sustainability but also a long-term financial strategy. As the demand for eco-friendly, resilient housing continues to grow, these homes are poised to increase in value, offering significant returns. Whether through energy savings, low maintenance costs, or market appreciation, earth-covered homes provide both environmental and financial benefits that make them a smart choice for the future.

Now that we've explored the financial advantages, let's dive into the day-to-day experience of living in an earth-covered home and how it impacts your lifestyle.

9

The Lifestyle of Living in an Earth-Covered Home

Living in an earth-covered home is like living within the earth's embrace—quiet, serene, and connected to the world around you. The experience of dwelling in a home nestled into the landscape is unlike any other. You feel insulated not only from the elements but also from the noise and chaos of the outside world. Every room is a refuge, a sanctuary of calm, where the temperature is stable, the air is fresh, and the connection to nature is ever-present.

In this chapter, we'll explore the unique lifestyle benefits of living in an earth-covered home, from the comfort of natural climate control to the health and psychological perks of living in a home designed to harmonize with the environment.

Comfort and Health Benefits

One of the most striking aspects of living in an earth-covered home is the **comfort** it provides in every season. These homes are naturally designed to regulate temperature, improve air quality, and create a peaceful, quiet living space. The result is not just a house that's energy-efficient but one that enhances both your physical and mental well-being.

1. Natural Climate Control Leads to Comfort in All Seasons

One of the key lifestyle benefits of earth-covered homes is their ability to maintain **consistent indoor temperatures** year-round. Because the home is surrounded by earth, the thick, insulating layers keep it cool in the summer and warm in the winter. Unlike traditional homes that can be susceptible to extreme heat or cold, earth-covered homes offer a **natural climate control system** that makes living spaces more comfortable.

The surrounding earth acts as a **thermal mass**, absorbing heat during the day and releasing it slowly at night. This leads to a more consistent temperature inside the home, reducing the need for artificial heating and cooling systems. The result is a space that feels cool and refreshing on a hot summer day and cozy during the winter months, all without the energy bills associated with conventional HVAC systems.

For many, this built-in climate control means more than just comfort—it means freedom from the fluctuations of extreme weather. Whether you live in a region with cold winters or scorching summers, an earth-covered home offers a stable, comfortable environment.

2. Health Benefits of Stable Temperatures, Reduced Allergens, and Improved Air Quality

In addition to comfort, earth-covered homes offer a range of **health benefits** that make them a healthier choice for homeowners. The combination of stable indoor temperatures, reduced exposure to outdoor pollutants, and improved indoor air quality can have a significant impact on overall well-being.

- **Stable Temperatures**: The consistent temperatures in earth-covered homes help reduce stress on the body. Unlike traditional homes where fluctuating temperatures can trigger respiratory issues or discomfort, the steady climate inside an earth-covered home is easier on the body, particularly for those with conditions like asthma or arthritis.
- **Reduced Allergens**: Because earth-covered homes are naturally insulated and sealed, they are less prone to **drafts** and **airborne allergens** that can make their way into traditional homes. Dust, pollen, and pollutants are kept at bay, creating a cleaner indoor environment.
- **Improved Air Quality**: With proper ventilation systems, such as **heat recovery ventilators (HRVs)** or **energy recovery ventilators (ERVs)**, earth-covered homes can maintain fresh air circulation without sacrificing energy efficiency. The result is better air quality and a reduced risk of mold, mildew, and airborne irritants, which can improve respiratory health.

3. Soundproofing Qualities That Create a Peaceful Living Environment

One of the unexpected joys of living in an earth-covered home is the **quiet** it offers. The thick layers of earth surrounding the home act as a natural sound barrier, blocking out noise from nearby roads, neighbors, or urban environments. Whether your home is located in a bustling city or a remote rural area, you'll notice a profound sense of **peace and tranquility** inside an earth-covered home.

This natural **soundproofing** creates a serene living environment, perfect for those who value silence, meditation, or simply a quiet place to relax. Unlike traditional homes where windows and walls can let in external noise, the earth surrounding an earth-covered home dampens sound, creating a cocoon-like atmosphere that enhances the feeling of privacy and calm.

The soundproofing qualities of earth-covered homes can be especially valuable for families or individuals who work from home, allowing for a more focused and peaceful work environment. It also benefits anyone who enjoys spending time in the quiet comfort of their home without the distractions of the outside world.

4. The Psychological Impact of Living Close to Nature

There's something inherently calming about being close to nature, and earth-covered homes offer a unique way to feel connected to the natural world. The design of these homes blends seamlessly into the surrounding landscape, offering large windows with views of greenery, green roofs, and sometimes even natural rock or earth visible from within the home. This connection to nature provides **psychological benefits** that go beyond aesthetics.

Living in an earth-covered home can improve mental health by reducing stress and promoting relaxation. The combination of **natural light**, **fresh air**, and a peaceful, quiet environment can have a profound impact on mood and mental well-being. Studies have shown that exposure to natural surroundings can reduce anxiety, improve focus, and enhance overall happiness. An earth-covered home, with its close connection to the earth and the elements, offers this experience on a daily basis.

Whether it's enjoying the view from a window, sitting in a courtyard garden, or simply knowing that your home is in harmony with the environment, living in an earth-covered home fosters a **sense of tranquility** and **mindful living**.

Story: A Family's First Year in an Earth-Covered Home and Their Newfound Sense of Peace

The Johnson family—Sarah, David, and their two children—made the decision to build an earth-covered home in the foothills of the Appalachian Mountains. They had always been drawn to sustainable living, but they didn't fully understand how much their new home would change their lives.

In the first few months, the family immediately noticed the **quiet**. After years of living in a busy neighborhood, they were amazed at how peaceful their home felt. The sounds of birds, wind, and distant rain became part of their daily life, while the noises of cars, lawnmowers, and city life were barely noticeable.

As the seasons changed, Sarah and David were struck by the home's **natural climate control**. The summer heatwaves that used to make their old home unbearable were no longer an issue. Their new earth-covered home stayed cool without air conditioning, thanks to the thermal mass of the surrounding earth. Winter brought a similar surprise: the home remained warm and cozy, with minimal need for heating. The temperature stayed so stable that they often forgot about the weather outside.

Perhaps the biggest surprise came when Sarah, who had long struggled with allergies, noticed a significant improvement in her symptoms. The home's **improved air quality** and lack of drafts made it easier for her to breathe, and her once-frequent sinus headaches became rare. The family also appreciated the **lack of dust and pollen** inside, which made cleaning easier and contributed to a healthier living environment.

By the end of their first year, the Johnsons realized that living in an earth-covered home had given them more than just energy savings and environmental benefits. It had provided them with a deeper sense of **peace**, a healthier lifestyle, and a home that felt truly connected to nature. "It's like the earth is protecting us," Sarah said. "We're part of the landscape now, and it's the most calming, comforting feeling."

Conclusion: Living in an earth-covered home offers a lifestyle that is comfortable, healthy, and deeply connected to the natural world. From natural climate control to improved air quality and the peace that comes with soundproofing and proximity to nature, these homes provide a unique experience that enhances both physical and mental well-being.

Now that we've explored the lifestyle benefits, let's shift focus to the financial returns. In the next chapter, we'll break down how earth-covered homes increase in value over time and provide long-term savings for homeowners

Designing for Modern Life

One of the most common misconceptions about earth-covered homes is that they might feel dark, confined, or even cave-like. In reality, these homes can be designed to be as modern, functional, and technologically advanced as any traditional home. By embracing contemporary design principles, flexible layouts, and innovative technology, earth-covered homes can cater to the needs of modern families while maintaining their sustainable, eco-friendly appeal.

Let's explore how you can design an earth-covered home that's not only energy-efficient and environmentally conscious but also perfectly suited for modern life, including flexible interiors, smart home technology, and spaces that blur the lines between indoors and outdoors.

1. Creating Functional, Modern Interiors That Don't Feel Like Caves

A well-designed earth-covered home should feel **bright**, **open**, and **welcoming**, not dark or closed off. By incorporating **strategic design elements**, such as natural lighting solutions, open floor plans, and carefully chosen materials, you can create interiors that feel spacious and contemporary.

Open Floor Plans and Flexible Spaces

One of the hallmarks of modern home design is the use of **open floor plans** that create a sense of flow between different areas of the home. In an earth-covered home, this is especially important to maximize the use of natural light and enhance the feeling of spaciousness.

- **Large, open living areas** that combine the kitchen, dining, and living spaces create an inviting, airy atmosphere. These spaces can be designed to have **floor-to-ceiling windows** on the exposed sides of the home, bringing in natural light and providing views of the surrounding landscape.
- **Flexible layouts** allow you to customize spaces according to your needs, whether it's creating a home office, a workout area, or an entertainment space. The key is to prioritize functionality and flow, ensuring that each room feels connected to the rest of the home.

Incorporating Natural Light

To avoid the feeling of being "buried" or confined, earth-covered homes often incorporate innovative **natural lighting solutions**, such as **skylights**, **solar tubes**, and **clerestory windows**. These elements flood the interior with light, making the home feel bright and cheerful.

- **Skylights** are particularly effective in earth-sheltered homes, where the roof is often the only surface directly exposed to the sky. They can be strategically placed in living rooms, kitchens, or even bathrooms to bring sunlight into deeper parts of the home.
- **Solar tubes** are another great option for bringing natural light into areas that are fully or partially underground. These tubes channel sunlight from outside into rooms that might otherwise be windowless, ensuring that every space feels well-lit and connected to the outdoors.

Natural Materials for Warmth and Texture

Choosing **natural materials** like wood, stone, and clay can enhance the warmth and aesthetic appeal of an earth-covered home. These materials not only create a connection to the environment but also add texture and character to the space. For example:

- **Wooden beams** and flooring can bring a sense of coziness and contrast to the sleek, minimalist design often found in modern interiors.
- **Exposed stone walls** can add a rugged, organic touch, reminding occupants that they are living within the earth while still feeling comfortable and sophisticated.

By carefully balancing modern design elements with natural materials and strategic lighting, earth-covered homes can be both functional and beautiful, without sacrificing the bright, open feel that many people crave in modern living spaces.

2. Incorporating Technology: Smart Homes and Earth-Covered Living

The modern home is no longer just a place to live—it's an integrated hub of technology designed to make life more convenient, efficient, and secure. **Smart home technology** can be seamlessly incorporated into an earth-covered home, enhancing its energy efficiency and creating a space that's both eco-friendly and tech-savvy.

Smart Energy Management

One of the major benefits of combining smart home technology with an earth-covered home is the ability to monitor and manage energy consumption in real time. Smart systems allow you to track and optimize your home's energy use, ensuring that you're getting the most out of the natural insulation and passive solar design of your earth-covered home.

- **Smart thermostats** can be programmed to adjust the temperature based on the time of day, weather conditions, or your daily routine. These systems ensure that you're using energy only when you need it, further reducing your utility bills.

- **Lighting automation** can be integrated with solar tubes and skylights, automatically adjusting artificial lighting levels as natural light changes throughout the day. This ensures your home is always well-lit without wasting electricity.

Home Security and Automation

Earth-covered homes, often built in rural or secluded locations, can benefit from **smart security systems** that allow homeowners to monitor and control their homes from anywhere. Whether it's through **smart door locks**, **security cameras**, or **motion sensors**, these systems provide peace of mind while blending seamlessly into the design of the home.

- **Voice-controlled home assistants** can also be integrated to control everything from lights and appliances to window shades and home security systems, making your earth-covered home as tech-savvy as any modern urban loft.

3. Flexible Layouts for Families, Work-from-Home Setups, and Entertainment Spaces

One of the biggest advantages of designing an earth-covered home from the ground up is the opportunity to create **flexible spaces** that meet the needs of modern life. Whether you're accommodating a growing family, setting up a home office, or creating a space for entertaining guests, earth-covered homes can be customized to fit your lifestyle.

Family-Friendly Designs

For families, it's important to design a home that's both functional and adaptable. Earth-covered homes can be designed with **multi-use rooms** that can change as the family's needs evolve. For example:

- **Open play areas** for young children can later be converted into study spaces or additional bedrooms as kids grow older.
- **Shared family spaces** like large living rooms or dining areas can be designed with flexibility in mind, allowing for easy reconfiguration when hosting gatherings or events.

Work-from-Home Setups

With the rise of remote work, many homeowners now need dedicated office space within their homes. Earth-covered homes can easily incorporate **quiet, well-lit office spaces** that are isolated from the main living areas, providing privacy and a peaceful work environment.

- Home offices in earth-covered homes can take advantage

of **natural light** from windows or skylights, ensuring a bright and productive workspace.
- The natural soundproofing qualities of earth-covered homes also make them ideal for creating a focused, distraction-free work environment.

Entertainment Spaces

For those who enjoy entertaining guests, earth-covered homes can include **dedicated entertainment spaces**, such as media rooms, home theaters, or game rooms. Thanks to the natural insulation provided by the surrounding earth, these spaces are often well-suited for soundproofing, making them perfect for hosting movie nights or parties without disturbing the rest of the household.

4. Outdoor-Indoor Living: Courtyards, Rooftop Gardens, and Natural Landscaping

One of the most exciting aspects of earth-covered homes is their ability to blend **indoor and outdoor living**. By integrating natural elements like courtyards, rooftop gardens, and native landscaping, you can create a home that feels connected to the earth in every way.

Courtyards

Courtyards act as natural light wells and ventilation systems, bringing daylight and fresh air into the heart of an earth-covered home. These open-air spaces can serve as **outdoor living rooms**, gardens, or even dining areas, providing a seamless transition between indoor and outdoor spaces.

- **Green walls** or trellises can enhance the natural feel of a courtyard, creating a space that feels lush and inviting.
- Courtyards can also function as **passive cooling systems**, allowing air to circulate through the home and naturally regulating the indoor temperature.

Rooftop Gardens

Rooftop gardens are a hallmark of earth-covered homes, offering both **aesthetic and environmental benefits**. These gardens not only add beauty to the home but also help insulate the roof and manage stormwater runoff.

- Rooftop gardens can be designed with **native plants** that require minimal maintenance and irrigation, further reducing the home's environmental impact.
- For those interested in growing their own food, **edible gardens** can be integrated into rooftop spaces, providing fresh produce while contributing to the home's sustainability.

Natural Landscaping

The landscaping around an earth-covered home is an extension of the home itself. By using **native plants** and **permaculture principles**, you can create a landscape that supports local ecosystems, conserves water, and enhances the natural beauty of the home.

- **Xeriscaping**, or designing landscapes that require little to no irrigation, is particularly effective for earth-covered homes in dry or arid climates.
- Pathways, terraces, and outdoor seating areas can be designed to feel organic and in harmony with the surrounding landscape, blurring the lines between the built environment and nature.

Case Study: A Tech-Savvy Family Who Integrated Smart Home Features into Their Earth-Sheltered Home

The Martins, a family of four, decided to build an earth-covered home in a suburban area, combining their love for technology with their desire for sustainable living. They were early adopters of **smart home technology** and wanted their new home to be as connected and efficient as possible.

Working with a designer who specialized in sustainable construction, they incorporated a range of smart home features, including:

- **Automated lighting and blinds**, which adjusted throughout the day based on natural light levels, reducing their energy consumption.
- **Voice-controlled systems** that allowed them to manage

their home's temperature, lighting, and security with simple voice commands.

- A **smart irrigation system** for their rooftop garden, which used weather data to determine when and how much to water, conserving water and keeping the garden lush year-round.

The Martins also made sure to design the home with flexible spaces for their growing children and their work-from-home needs. Over the years, the family found that their earth-covered home not only provided a **high-tech, eco-friendly lifestyle** but also offered the peace and connection to nature that they had longed for.

Conclusion: Designing an earth-covered home for modern life means embracing the best of both worlds—combining the **comforts of advanced technology** with the **peace and sustainability of nature**. From smart homes and flexible layouts to courtyards and rooftop gardens, these homes offer endless possibilities for creating a space that meets the needs of today's families while staying connected to the earth.

Now that we've explored the ways to design for modern living, let's delve into the lifestyle of living in an earth-covered home and how it enhances daily life in profound and unexpected ways.

Integrating with the Local Community

Building and living in an earth-covered home doesn't mean isolating yourself from the world around you. In fact, these homes can fit seamlessly into neighborhoods and urban landscapes, providing a model for sustainable living that others in the community can appreciate and even adopt. Whether you're part of a bustling city, a suburban neighborhood, or an eco-village, earth-covered homes offer an opportunity to integrate **sustainability** into the local community in meaningful ways.

In this section, we'll explore how earth-covered homes fit into different types of communities, from urban neighborhoods to **eco-villages** and **cohousing communities**. We'll also look at how homeowners can get involved in local sustainability efforts, from participating in **community gardens** to educating neighbors about the benefits of eco-friendly living.

1. How Earth-Covered Homes Fit into Neighborhoods and Urban Landscapes

While earth-covered homes are often associated with rural settings, they are increasingly being integrated into **urban and suburban landscapes**, offering an alternative to traditional housing. These homes blend naturally into their surroundings, making them suitable for a wide range of environments, from city centers to residential neighborhoods.

Fitting into Urban Environments

In urban areas where space is limited and density is high, earth-covered homes can offer a unique solution. By building partially or fully underground, these homes can maximize the use of land without disrupting the natural landscape or blocking views. **Green roofs** and **bermed earth** allow the home to blend into parks, public spaces, or existing infrastructure, creating a seamless connection between the built environment and nature.

For example:

- **Earth-sheltered homes** in urban areas can incorporate **rooftop gardens** that function as green spaces for the neighborhood, providing a habitat for wildlife, reducing the urban heat island effect, and improving air quality.
- In residential areas, earth-covered homes can be designed to fit within the existing architectural styles while still maintaining their eco-friendly, energy-efficient features. By using natural materials like stone, wood, and glass, these homes can complement their surroundings rather than standing out as unconventional.

Suburban Integration

In suburban neighborhoods, earth-covered homes can be designed to blend seamlessly into **natural landscapes** while offering privacy and energy efficiency. The homes' low profile and natural insulation mean they have a minimal impact on their surroundings, preserving the neighborhood's character while offering a sustainable alternative to traditional suburban housing.

- Earth-covered homes can be designed with **large windows** facing open spaces like backyards, allowing homeowners to enjoy a connection to nature while maintaining a sense of privacy.
- By incorporating **sustainable landscaping** practices, such as rain gardens and xeriscaping, these homes can also contribute to neighborhood efforts to conserve water and reduce the environmental impact of suburban living.

2. Earth-Covered Homes in Eco-Villages and Cohousing Communities

One of the most exciting movements in sustainable living is the rise of **eco-villages** and **cohousing communities**, where residents work together to create a way of life that prioritizes environmental responsibility, social interaction, and resource-sharing. Earth-covered homes are a perfect fit for these communities, offering a model for energy-efficient, low-impact living.

Eco-Villages: A Model of Sustainable Living

In **eco-villages**, residents focus on living in harmony with nature, often using renewable energy, growing their own food, and minimizing waste. Earth-covered homes are ideal for these settings because they naturally align with the goals of

self-sufficiency and **low-impact living**.

- Homes in eco-villages are often built using **local materials** and designed to blend into the natural landscape, reducing the need for artificial heating and cooling.
- The energy savings and reduced maintenance of earth-covered homes make them a smart choice for residents who want to live sustainably without relying heavily on external resources.

Cohousing Communities: Shared Spaces, Shared Values

In **cohousing communities**, homeowners live in private residences but share common spaces such as kitchens, gardens, and recreational areas. Earth-covered homes work well in these communities because they support the core principles of **resource sharing** and **community engagement**.

- Earth-covered homes in cohousing communities can incorporate **shared green spaces** on rooftops or bermed areas, creating communal gardens or gathering spaces that encourage social interaction and sustainability.
- By sharing **renewable energy systems**, such as solar panels or geothermal heating, cohousing communities with earth-covered homes can further reduce their collective environmental impact.

Both eco-villages and cohousing communities provide a supportive environment for earth-covered homes, making them an excellent option for homeowners looking to live sustainably while being part of a close-knit, environmentally-conscious community.

3. Participating in Local Sustainability Efforts (Community Gardens, Green Spaces)

Living in an earth-covered home often inspires homeowners to get involved in **local sustainability initiatives**. Many communities are working to reduce their environmental impact by creating **community gardens**, preserving green spaces, and implementing eco-friendly practices, and earth-covered homeowners can play a key role in these efforts.

Community Gardens

Community gardens are a great way to engage with neighbors while promoting local food production and sustainability. Earth-covered homeowners, who often have a deep connection to the land, can use their knowledge of **sustainable gardening practices**—such as permaculture, water conservation, and composting—to contribute to these shared spaces.

- Community gardens offer an opportunity to **share resources** and knowledge with neighbors, from growing food to managing soil health.
- Earth-covered homeowners can also participate in efforts to create **rooftop or courtyard gardens** that bring greenery into urban or suburban areas, improving air quality and fostering a sense of community.

Preserving and Creating Green Spaces

Another way to contribute to local sustainability is by participating in efforts to **preserve green spaces** and **create natural areas** in your community. Earth-covered homes, with their green roofs and natural landscaping, can serve as examples of how to integrate **biodiversity** into residential areas without sacrificing space for homes.

- By working with local governments or environmental organizations, earth-covered homeowners can advocate for more **green roofs** on public buildings, encourage the creation of **wildlife corridors**, and support the preservation of **natural habitats** in urban environments.
- Homeowners can also lead by example, showcasing how **sustainable landscaping**—such as using native plants, reducing water consumption, and eliminating pesticides— can benefit the entire community.

4. Educating Neighbors and Promoting Sustainable Living

Owning an earth-covered home places you in a unique position to **educate others** about the benefits of sustainable living. While these homes are becoming more popular, many people are still unfamiliar with their advantages and might not understand how eco-friendly homes can benefit the larger community.

Hosting Educational Events and Open Houses

One way to share your knowledge and passion for sustainable

living is by hosting **educational events** or **open houses** for neighbors and community members. These events can provide an opportunity to:

- Showcase the **energy efficiency** and **environmental benefits** of your earth-covered home.
- Share information on **renewable energy systems**, such as solar panels or geothermal heating, and how they can be integrated into traditional homes.
- Offer advice on **sustainable practices** that anyone can adopt, such as composting, rainwater harvesting, or native landscaping.

Collaborating with Local Schools or Environmental Groups

Another way to promote sustainability is by collaborating with local **schools**, **universities**, or **environmental groups** to share the benefits of earth-covered homes. Whether it's through giving a presentation to students or working with a local green building group, you can help spread awareness of eco-friendly construction and inspire others to consider **sustainable housing** options.

Promoting Policy Changes

Homeowners with earth-covered homes can also advocate for **policy changes** that encourage sustainable building practices in their communities. By working with local governments or sustainability organizations, you can help push for **incentives** for green building, such as tax breaks for energy-efficient homes or requirements for more sustainable construction practices in new developments.

Case Study: A Community of Earth-Covered Homes That Became a Model for Urban Sustainability

In the early 2000s, a group of environmentally-conscious architects and homeowners came together to create **Greenridge**, a community of earth-covered homes in a mid-sized urban area. The goal was to build homes that minimized energy use, blended seamlessly with the natural landscape, and promoted sustainability within the broader community.

The residents of Greenridge collaborated with local government officials to create a neighborhood that emphasized **green spaces**, **renewable energy**, and **community-driven sustainability efforts**. Each home was built with **green roofs**, **solar panels**, and **natural insulation**, reducing the community's overall carbon footprint.

Over time, Greenridge became a **model for urban sustainability**, attracting interest from architects, environmental groups, and city planners. The community's focus on **low-impact living** inspired the surrounding neighborhood to adopt similar practices, from establishing community gardens to encouraging the use of renewable energy in public buildings.

Greenridge's success didn't stop there. The community hosted **educational workshops** for local residents, showcasing the benefits of earth-covered homes and eco-friendly practices. Today, Greenridge is recognized as a trailblazer in the movement toward **urban sustainability**, demonstrating that earth-covered homes can thrive in urban environments while leading the way in eco-friendly living.

Conclusion: Integrating an earth-covered home into the local community offers the opportunity to lead by example, showing how sustainable living can benefit not just individuals but the neighborhood as a whole. From fitting into urban landscapes to contributing to eco-villages, earth-covered homes are part of a growing movement toward environmentally-conscious living that prioritizes both comfort and community.

Now that you've learned about the lifestyle benefits of earth-covered homes, let's explore the **legal and regulatory aspects** of building one. Understanding these details will help ensure that your project runs smoothly from start to finish

10

Legal and Zoning Considerations

"**C**an you legally bury your house in your city?" This question might seem like an odd one, but it's one of the first things you'll need to ask if you're considering building an earth-covered home. While these eco-friendly, innovative structures offer a range of benefits, they also bring unique legal and zoning challenges that must be addressed early in the planning process. Building an earth-covered home involves more than just construction—it requires navigating local laws, zoning restrictions, and building codes that may not have been designed with underground or earth-sheltered homes in mind.

In this chapter, we'll explore the **legal considerations** you'll need to address when building an earth-covered home, including zoning laws, building codes, and how to work with city planners and architects to ensure your home complies with local regulations.

Zoning and Building Codes

Before you start construction on your earth-covered home, it's essential to understand the **zoning laws** and **building codes** in your area. These regulations vary widely depending on your location and can significantly impact the design and feasibility of your project. While some areas may welcome innovative, sustainable designs, others may have strict rules that make it difficult to build an earth-covered home without special permits or variances.

Local Zoning Laws That Affect Earth-Covered Homes

Zoning laws are local regulations that govern land use, dictating what types of buildings can be constructed in specific areas and how they must be built. These laws determine everything from how tall a building can be to how far it must be set back from the property line. For earth-covered homes, zoning laws can present unique challenges because these homes don't always fit the mold of traditional housing.

- **Height Restrictions**: In some areas, zoning laws set height limits for homes, which can be beneficial for earth-covered homes since they often have low profiles or are built partially underground. However, in other cases, the unique design of an earth-covered home—especially if it includes berms or is integrated into the landscape—may require zoning adjustments.
- **Setback Requirements**: Many municipalities have **setback regulations** that dictate how far your home must be from property lines, roads, or other structures. Earth-covered

homes, particularly those that incorporate berms or green roofs, may need special consideration if their design encroaches on these required setbacks.

- **Land Use**: In some areas, certain types of housing are restricted by **land use laws**. For example, earth-covered homes might be considered "unconventional" and not allowed in areas zoned for single-family homes. In this case, you may need to apply for a variance or lobby for zoning changes.

Understanding Building Codes for Non-Traditional Structures

Building codes are another critical factor to consider when planning an earth-covered home. These codes set the minimum standards for construction, including structural integrity, electrical systems, plumbing, and fire safety. For non-traditional homes like earth-covered structures, complying with these codes can be more challenging because they are often designed with conventional above-ground homes in mind.

- **Structural Safety**: Earth-covered homes require special attention to **structural safety** due to the weight of the earth surrounding the structure. Building codes may require that your home meet specific **load-bearing** standards to ensure the walls and roof can support the additional weight. You may need to work with a structural engineer to demonstrate that your home will meet these requirements.
- **Ventilation and Moisture Control**: Building codes also require proper **ventilation** and **moisture control** to prevent

mold, mildew, and other issues that can arise in earth-covered homes. Ensuring your design includes systems that allow for adequate airflow and moisture management is critical to getting approval from local building inspectors.

- **Fire Safety**: Fire safety codes may also need to be addressed differently in an earth-covered home. While these homes are naturally more fire-resistant due to their design and materials, you'll still need to comply with local fire codes, which may include requirements for **egress windows**, smoke detectors, and fire-rated building materials.

Navigating Challenges in Urban Areas

Building an earth-covered home in an urban area can come with additional challenges. Cities often have stricter **zoning laws** and **building codes** than rural or suburban areas, and the dense population may make it more difficult to get approval for non-traditional housing.

- **Land Availability**: Finding suitable land for an earth-covered home in an urban area can be difficult. The limited availability of lots, combined with zoning laws that favor high-density housing, may require you to be creative in your design or seek exceptions to the rules.
- **Excavation and Infrastructure**: Earth-covered homes often require extensive excavation, which can be more complicated and costly in urban environments. Additionally, you'll need to ensure that your home doesn't interfere with existing **infrastructure**, such as underground utilities, sewer lines, or electrical systems.

- **Working with City Planners**: One of the best ways to navigate the complexities of building an earth-covered home in an urban area is to work closely with **city planners**. These professionals can help you understand the local regulations, identify potential obstacles, and guide you through the permitting process.

Working with Architects and City Planners to Ensure Compliance

Building an earth-covered home requires a team effort. To ensure your home complies with all local laws and regulations, it's essential to work with **experienced architects**, **city planners**, and **engineers** who understand the unique challenges of these homes. Their expertise can help you navigate the approval process and ensure your project meets all legal requirements.

Finding an Architect with Earth-Covered Home Experience

Not all architects have experience designing earth-covered homes, so it's crucial to find someone who understands the unique construction techniques and legal requirements. An experienced architect can help you:

- Design a home that complies with local **building codes** while still achieving your sustainability goals.
- Work with city planners and building inspectors to ensure

that your design is approved without delays.

- Address any concerns about **structural integrity**, **ventilation**, and **fire safety** before construction begins.

Collaborating with City Planners and Engineers

City planners and engineers are often involved in the permitting process for non-traditional homes. By collaborating with these professionals early in the design phase, you can:

- Identify any **zoning issues** or building code challenges that may need to be addressed before construction.
- Apply for **variances** or **special permits** if your home doesn't fit within the existing zoning regulations.
- Ensure that your home meets all **structural** and **environmental** requirements, including load-bearing capacity and stormwater management.

Case Study: A Homeowner Who Successfully Lobbied for Zoning Changes

In 2015, **Karen**, an environmentally-conscious homeowner, wanted to build an earth-covered home in a suburban neighborhood near Boulder, Colorado. She loved the idea of living sustainably but quickly discovered that her local **zoning laws** prohibited earth-covered structures. The area was zoned for traditional single-family homes, and her design didn't comply with the height or setback restrictions.

Rather than giving up on her dream, Karen decided to take action. She began attending **city council meetings** and engaging with local officials to explain the benefits of earth-covered homes. Karen emphasized the **environmental benefits**, including reduced energy consumption, natural stormwater management, and the preservation of green space. She also brought in architects and engineers to demonstrate that her home would meet all structural and safety requirements.

After months of lobbying and providing evidence that her home would be an asset to the community, Karen was granted a zoning variance. She successfully built her earth-covered home, which not only met all local regulations but also became a model for other homeowners interested in sustainable living. Her efforts helped change local attitudes toward alternative housing, paving the way for future projects in the area.

Conclusion: Building an earth-covered home requires more than just a vision for sustainable living—it also requires navigating local zoning laws, building codes, and regulatory hurdles. By working closely with architects, engineers, and city planners, you can ensure that your home meets all legal requirements and overcomes any obstacles. With the right approach, you can turn your dream of living in an earth-covered home into a reality.

Now that we've covered the legal and regulatory aspects of building an earth-covered home, let's dive into the **financing options** and incentives available to help fund your eco-friendly project.

Permits and Approvals

Once you've navigated the zoning laws and building codes, the next step in building your earth-covered home is securing the necessary **permits and approvals**. This process is crucial to ensure your project meets local regulations, adheres to environmental standards, and is built safely and efficiently. While the permitting process for traditional homes is often straightforward, earth-covered homes may require additional approvals, particularly for **grading**, **excavation**, and **water management**. In some cases, you'll also need to work with environmental agencies and **eco-certification bodies** to ensure your home meets sustainability standards.

In this section, we'll guide you through the key permits you'll need, how to work with environmental agencies, and how eco-certifications can benefit your project. We'll also walk through a real-world example of securing permits for an earth-sheltered home.

1. Key Permits Needed for Construction (Grading, Excavation, Water Management)

The permitting process for an earth-covered home often involves more steps than a traditional home due to the unique nature of its construction. Here's a breakdown of the key permits you'll likely need to secure before beginning construction:

1. Grading and Excavation Permits

Since earth-covered homes often involve significant excavation to build into the landscape or create berms, you'll need a **grading and excavation permit**. This permit ensures that your plans for reshaping the land—whether you're digging into a hillside or piling earth over a structure—comply with local safety and environmental regulations.

- **Grading Permits**: Grading involves reshaping the land to suit the design of your home. The local authorities will review your plans to ensure that the grading doesn't cause **erosion**, **landslides**, or **drainage issues** for nearby properties. Grading permits are especially important in areas with steep terrain or unstable soils.
- **Excavation Permits**: Excavation refers to the removal of earth to create space for your home. This is common in earth-sheltered designs where the structure is partially or fully underground. You'll need to provide detailed plans showing the depth of excavation, the amount of soil to be removed, and how the excavated material will be managed or reused on-site. Some municipalities may also require you to conduct a **soil stability** test to ensure the land can

support an underground home without risk of collapse or shifting.

2. Water Management and Drainage Permits

Proper **water management** is critical for any home, but it's especially important for earth-covered homes due to their interaction with the surrounding soil. You'll need to obtain permits that address how your home will manage **stormwater**, **groundwater**, and **drainage** to prevent flooding or erosion.

- **Stormwater Management Permits**: Stormwater management involves controlling the runoff from rainfall or snowmelt. For earth-covered homes, you'll need to demonstrate that your design includes systems to handle excess water, such as **French drains**, **retaining walls**, or **drainage swales**. These systems must prevent water from pooling around the foundation or eroding the landscape.
- **Drainage Plans**: Some municipalities will require a detailed **drainage plan** as part of the permitting process. This plan shows how water will flow around your home and how you'll prevent water from affecting neighboring properties or public infrastructure. It may also need to account for **rainwater harvesting** systems, which are commonly incorporated into earth-covered homes to enhance sustainability.

3. Building Permits

Once you've secured your grading, excavation, and water management permits, you'll need a **building permit**. This is the most comprehensive permit, covering the construction of the home itself. It ensures that your home meets local **structural**, **electrical**, **plumbing**, and **fire safety** codes. For an earth-covered home, you may need to provide additional documentation demonstrating that the structure can withstand the weight of the surrounding earth and maintain proper ventilation.

2. Getting Approval from Environmental Agencies

Building an earth-covered home often means interacting with the natural landscape in ways that traditional homes do not, which can trigger the need for additional approvals from **environmental agencies**. These agencies ensure that your project doesn't negatively impact local ecosystems, water sources, or wildlife. Working closely with these agencies can help you design a home that is both environmentally friendly and compliant with local regulations.

1. Wetlands and Protected Areas

If your property is near a **wetland**, **river**, or **protected habitat**, you may need approval from local or federal environmental agencies, such as the **Environmental Protection Agency (EPA)** in the U.S. or similar bodies in other countries. These agencies will review your project to ensure it doesn't harm sensitive ecosystems or disrupt water sources.

- **Wetland Permits**: If your home is near or in a wetland area, you'll need a permit to ensure that your construction won't disturb the wetlands or affect their ability to filter water and support wildlife. Earth-covered homes, which often have minimal environmental footprints, are typically well-received by environmental agencies, but careful planning is still required.

2. Tree Removal and Vegetation Impact

Many municipalities require permits for the removal of **trees** or other vegetation, particularly if you're building in a forested or environmentally sensitive area. Since earth-covered homes often involve reshaping the landscape, you'll need to demonstrate that your construction plan minimizes the impact on local flora and fauna.

- **Replanting and Landscaping Plans**: To offset the environmental impact of tree removal or excavation, you may be required to submit a **replanting plan** that outlines how you'll restore vegetation after construction. Many earth-covered homes integrate **green roofs** or **native landscaping** into their design, which can satisfy these requirements.

3. Wildlife Protection

In areas where endangered or protected species live, you may need to consult with environmental agencies to ensure your project doesn't harm local wildlife. These agencies may require **environmental impact assessments** before construction can begin.

- **Habitat Protection Plans**: If your property is home to protected species, you may need to develop a **habitat protection plan** that outlines how your construction will avoid disrupting their environment. This can include adjusting the location of your home on the property, limiting construction to certain times of the year, or incorporating features that support wildlife, such as natural corridors.

3. Working with Eco-Certification Bodies for Sustainable Building Standards

While obtaining the necessary permits and approvals is crucial, working with **eco-certification bodies** can provide additional benefits by verifying that your home meets recognized **sustainable building standards**. These certifications not only enhance your home's environmental performance but can also increase its market value and make you eligible for **green building incentives**.

1. LEED Certification

LEED (Leadership in Energy and Environmental Design) is one of the most widely recognized green building certification programs. LEED-certified homes must meet stringent criteria for energy efficiency, water conservation, indoor air quality, and sustainable materials.

- **Benefits of LEED Certification**: Achieving LEED certification can make your earth-covered home more attractive to eco-conscious buyers and may qualify you for **tax incentives** or **rebates** offered by local governments for sustainable building projects.

2. Passive House Certification

Passive House is another certification focused on extreme energy efficiency. Homes certified under the Passive House standard must meet strict energy performance requirements, such as reduced heating and cooling needs, superior insulation, and airtight construction.

- **Energy Efficiency and Comfort**: Earth-covered homes are naturally suited to achieve Passive House certification due to their superior insulation and low energy demands for heating and cooling. Passive House certification can be a major selling point, as it signifies that the home is built to perform at the highest levels of energy efficiency.

3. Net-Zero Energy Certification

For those aiming to build a home that produces as much energy as it consumes, **Net-Zero Energy Certification** is the ultimate goal. This certification ensures that your home generates renewable energy (through solar, wind, or other sources) that offsets its total energy consumption.

- **Net-Zero Potential of Earth-Covered Homes**: The design of earth-covered homes, which already minimizes energy use through passive solar heating and natural insulation, makes them ideal candidates for achieving **net-**

zero energy. By integrating solar panels, wind turbines, or geothermal systems, your home could meet the rigorous standards for this certification.

4. Example: The Step-by-Step Process of Securing Permits for an Earth-Sheltered Home

John and Lisa, a couple living in upstate New York, decided to build an earth-sheltered home on a piece of rural land they had purchased. Here's how they navigated the process of securing permits and approvals for their dream home.

Step 1: Initial Research and Consultation

John and Lisa began by consulting with an **architect** who specialized in earth-covered homes. The architect advised them to start with a thorough understanding of local zoning laws and building codes. They also hired a **civil engineer** to assess the land's topography and drainage patterns.

Step 2: Securing Grading and Excavation Permits

Since their home would be partially built into a hillside, the couple applied for a **grading and excavation permit**. They worked with their engineer to create a detailed grading plan that showed how the land would be reshaped without causing erosion or affecting nearby properties. The permit was approved after a few revisions to ensure the project wouldn't interfere with the local watershed.

Step 3: Water Management Approvals

Next, they applied for a **stormwater management permit**, demonstrating how their home's green roof and French drain system would handle runoff. The local planning board required them to submit a **drainage plan**, showing how water would flow away from the home during heavy rains. After consulting with an environmental engineer, the couple's plan was approved.

Step 4: Building Permit and Environmental Approvals

With their excavation and water management permits secured, John and Lisa applied for a **building permit**. This permit included reviews of the home's structural integrity, fire safety, and ventilation systems. Since their property bordered a small wetland, they also worked with the **local environmental agency** to ensure their construction wouldn't harm the wetland ecosystem. This involved slightly adjusting the location of the home to create a buffer zone around the wetland.

Step 5: Achieving LEED Certification

Finally, the couple decided to pursue **LEED certification** to maximize the sustainability of their home. They worked closely with their architect and builder to ensure that the home met the criteria for energy efficiency, water conservation, and indoor air quality. After construction was complete, their home was awarded **LEED Gold certification**, a major achievement that validated their commitment to sustainability.

Conclusion: Navigating the permitting process for an earth-covered home can be complex, but with careful planning, it's entirely manageable. By securing the right permits for grading, excavation, water management, and building, and working with environmental agencies and eco-certification bodies, you can ensure that your project is both legally compliant and environmentally responsible.

Now that you understand the legal and regulatory requirements, let's explore the next step—**budgeting and financing** your earth-covered home to turn your vision into reality.

Overcoming Regulatory Barriers

Building an earth-covered home comes with exciting opportunities but also a few regulatory challenges. While sustainable living is gaining traction worldwide, many local governments and planning departments still operate under **outdated building codes** that are not designed to accommodate non-traditional structures like earth-covered homes. These regulatory barriers can be frustrating, but with the right approach, they can be overcome.

In this section, we'll discuss the **common obstacles** you might face when trying to build an earth-covered home, provide examples of successful advocacy for sustainable housing, and offer tips on how to engage with local governments to get the necessary approvals. We'll also touch on the legal considerations for **off-grid or autonomous earth homes**, providing a roadmap to help you turn potential roadblocks into opportunities for progress.

1. Common Obstacles and How to Overcome Them (Outdated Building Codes)

When building an earth-covered home, one of the most frequent challenges you'll encounter is dealing with **outdated building codes** that weren't designed with modern sustainable homes in mind. Many existing regulations are tailored to traditional stick-built homes and may not account for the unique construction, materials, or environmental benefits of earth-covered structures. Here are some of the most common obstacles and how to overcome them:

Obstacle 1: Structural Integrity Requirements

Many building codes require that homes meet specific structural standards, particularly regarding **load-bearing capacity** and **foundation design**. These standards are often based on conventional above-ground construction, which doesn't consider the unique properties of earth-covered homes.

Solution:

To overcome this obstacle, work with a **structural engineer** who has experience designing earth-sheltered homes. They can help you create a design that demonstrates your home's ability to withstand the weight of the surrounding earth and meet all safety requirements. In some cases, you may need to provide additional documentation, such as a soil stability report or detailed load calculations, to satisfy building inspectors.

Obstacle 2: Ventilation and Moisture Control Standards

Because earth-covered homes are partially or fully under-ground, many local codes may require enhanced **ventilation** and **moisture control** measures to ensure that the home remains habitable and mold-free. While these concerns are valid, modern earth-covered homes are typically designed with these factors in mind.

Solution:

Incorporating **heat recovery ventilators (HRVs)** or **energy recovery ventilators (ERVs)** can provide the necessary airflow without sacrificing energy efficiency. To overcome this regulatory barrier, show local officials how your home will meet or exceed ventilation requirements through the use of modern systems. Additionally, ensure your design includes effective **waterproofing** and **drainage systems** to address any concerns about moisture buildup.

Obstacle 3: Building Height Restrictions and Setbacks

Some areas have strict rules about **building height** and **setback distances** from property lines. Earth-covered homes often have a lower profile than traditional homes, but depending on the local codes, their unique design (including berms or green roofs) may still require special consideration.

Solution:

If your earth-covered home design conflicts with height restrictions or setback rules, you may need to apply for a **variance**—a special exception that allows you to build in a way that deviates from the norm. Variances are typically granted when a homeowner can demonstrate that their proposed design won't negatively impact neighbors or the surrounding environment. For earth-covered homes, the **low visual impact** and **environmental benefits** often work in your favor when applying for a variance.

2. Examples of Successful Advocacy for Sustainable Homes

There are numerous examples of homeowners and builders successfully advocating for changes to local building codes to accommodate sustainable homes, including earth-covered structures. These cases show that while the process may require persistence, local governments are increasingly open to new, eco-friendly designs that promote energy efficiency and sustainability.

Example 1: The Earth Home Advocacy Group in California

In 2018, a group of eco-conscious builders in California sought to build a small community of earth-covered homes in a suburban area. The local building codes didn't allow for underground homes, and the required insulation and ventilation standards were designed for traditional houses. Rather than giving up, the group organized an advocacy campaign to educate local officials about the **energy-saving benefits** of earth-covered homes.

They hosted **community workshops**, provided case studies of successful earth-covered homes from around the world, and collaborated with environmental organizations to showcase the **carbon reduction** potential of these homes. After months of discussions and presentations, the local council agreed to update the building codes to include specific provisions for earth-sheltered homes, making the community project possible.

Example 2: The Green Ridge Initiative

In a small town in Oregon, a builder named **Samantha** faced resistance when trying to construct earth-covered homes in a neighborhood zoned for traditional houses. The local planning commission was concerned about whether the homes would fit with the character of the neighborhood and comply with safety standards. Samantha approached this challenge by working closely with local architects and engineers to develop a **building code amendment** specific to earth-covered homes.

By focusing on the benefits these homes would bring to the community—such as **reduced energy consumption**, **improved stormwater management**, and **increased property values**—she persuaded the commission to allow a pilot project. The success of that first earth-covered home led to more interest, and the town ultimately revised its building codes to allow for sustainable homes like Samantha's to be built in residential areas.

3. How to Approach Local Government with Proposals for Earth-Covered Homes

If you're planning to build an earth-covered home and face resistance or uncertainty from your local government, there are several steps you can take to effectively advocate for your project. Engaging with city officials, building inspectors, and community members is key to overcoming regulatory hurdles and ensuring that your home is approved.

Step 1: Do Your Homework

Before approaching local officials, do your research. Understand the current zoning laws and building codes in your area and identify any potential obstacles to your project. Gather **case studies** of successful earth-covered homes, particularly those in areas with similar climates or local regulations.

- Review local ordinances to see if there are any existing provisions for **sustainable housing** or **non-traditional homes**.
- Compile information about the **environmental benefits** and **energy savings** associated with earth-covered homes. Many local governments are more open to projects that align with their sustainability goals.

Step 2: Prepare a Detailed Proposal

When you meet with local officials, come prepared with a detailed proposal that explains your project in depth. Include **architectural plans**, **engineering reports**, and a thorough explanation of how your home will meet or exceed local safety and environmental standards.

- Be sure to address any concerns about **structural integrity**, **moisture control**, and **ventilation** upfront. Providing solutions in your initial proposal will help build confidence in your project.
- Emphasize the long-term **energy savings** and **environmental impact** of your earth-covered home. Local governments are often looking for ways to reduce their carbon

footprint, and your home can be part of that solution.

Step 3: Engage the Community

Involving your neighbors and the broader community can be an important step in gaining support for your earth-covered home. Hosting informational sessions, open houses, or workshops can help demystify earth-covered homes and show their benefits.

- Consider organizing a **neighborhood meeting** where you can explain your project and address any concerns about how it might affect the community. Highlight the low visual impact, environmental benefits, and energy efficiency of earth-covered homes.
- If your local government allows for public comment on building projects, encourage community members who support sustainable housing to voice their approval.

Step 4: Be Persistent and Open to Compromise

Navigating local regulations can be a long process, but persistence often pays off. Be prepared to engage in multiple meetings with local officials and make adjustments to your design if necessary. Flexibility is key—sometimes, small changes to your plans (such as adjusting the setback distance or modifying the roof design) can make a big difference in gaining approval.

4. Legal Considerations for Off-Grid or Autonomous Earth Homes

For those building earth-covered homes with the goal of living **off-grid** or creating an autonomous home, there are additional legal considerations to keep in mind. Off-grid living often involves generating your own power, managing your own water supply, and handling waste independently of municipal systems. While this offers incredible freedom and sustainability, it can also introduce legal challenges. **_(I have a full guide to off grid living which goes into this in full detail-look it up if you're interested!)_**

Power Generation and Utility Disconnects

Many local governments require homes to be connected to public utilities for safety and oversight purposes. If you plan to power your earth-covered home with **solar panels**, **wind turbines**, or **geothermal energy**, you'll need to ensure that your system meets local safety standards and codes.

- **Utility Requirements**: Some areas have regulations that mandate homes remain connected to the grid even if they generate their own power. Research these rules early to determine whether you can legally disconnect from public utilities, or if you'll need to maintain a minimal connection to comply with local laws.

Water Rights and Management

For homes that rely on **rainwater harvesting** or **well water**, there may be restrictions on how you can collect and use water. In some regions, water rights are tightly controlled, and you may need special permits to install a rainwater catchment system or well.

- **Septic and Waste Management**: If you plan to use a **composting toilet** or other non-traditional waste systems, make sure these systems comply with local health and safety codes. Some areas may require additional inspections or certifications for alternative waste management systems.

Story: A Builder Who Changed Local Laws to Accommodate Earth-Covered Homes

Michael, an innovative builder in the Pacific Northwest, became passionate about earth-covered homes after building his first one on a friend's rural property. He loved the idea of bringing sustainable, energy-efficient homes into more populated areas, but quickly encountered roadblocks when he tried to build similar homes in suburban neighborhoods. The local building codes didn't allow for underground homes, and there was skepticism from city planners about the feasibility of his designs.

Rather than giving up, Michael decided to take a proactive approach. He began working with local environmental groups and presented the idea of earth-covered homes to the city council, emphasizing their **sustainability**, **energy savings**, and **minimal environmental impact**. He also connected with engineers and architects who helped draft new building code provisions that specifically addressed the unique needs of earth-covered homes.

After two years of advocacy, Michael succeeded in getting the city to update its building codes to allow for earth-covered homes in residential areas. His persistence not only made it possible for him to build his dream homes but also opened the door for others in the community to explore sustainable housing options.

Conclusion: Overcoming regulatory barriers to build an earth-covered home requires persistence, creativity, and a willingness to engage with local governments and communities. By understanding the challenges, preparing detailed proposals, and advocating for sustainable housing, you can successfully navigate the legal landscape and bring your vision to life.

You're almost ready—let's take a look at some inspiring examples of earth-covered homes from around the world and see how they're redefining modern living.

11

Inspiring Earth-Covered Homes Around the World

"**A**rchitecture should not disrupt the earth, but become part of it," said Swiss architect Peter Vetsch, a pioneer in the field of **earth-sheltered architecture**. His philosophy captures the essence of earth-covered homes—buildings that don't stand apart from the natural world but rather blend seamlessly into it. Across the globe, architects and homeowners are embracing this idea, creating earth-covered homes that are as functional as they are beautiful, drawing inspiration from their surroundings and making a positive impact on the environment.

In this chapter, we'll explore some of the most inspiring earth-covered homes around the world, examining how different cultures, climates, and architectural styles have shaped their design. From Hobbit-inspired homes in New Zealand to modern eco-houses in Scandinavia, these homes are redefining what it means to live in harmony with nature.

Iconic Earth-Covered Homes

Earth-covered homes come in many shapes, sizes, and styles, reflecting not only the individual preferences of their creators but also the environmental and cultural contexts in which they are built. Let's take a closer look at some of the most iconic earth-covered homes across the globe, and how they've influenced sustainable architecture.

1. The Earth House Estate by Peter Vetsch (Switzerland)

One of the most famous collections of earth-covered homes is the **Earth House Estate** in Dietikon, Switzerland, designed by Peter Vetsch. These homes are instantly recognizable for their organic, rounded shapes that seem to flow out of the landscape itself. Built into the earth, the homes are covered with soil and vegetation, making them nearly invisible from above and creating a seamless integration with the surrounding countryside.

Vetsch's design philosophy revolves around the idea that architecture should not dominate the landscape but work in harmony with it. His earth houses use natural insulation provided by the surrounding earth to create energy-efficient living spaces, reducing the need for artificial heating and cooling. The homes also feature **curved walls** and **natural materials**, creating a soft, welcoming interior that feels closer to nature than traditional homes.

- **Design Influence:** Vetsch's designs have influenced architects around the world who are interested in creating homes that blend into the landscape rather than stand apart from it. His use of rounded, organic shapes has become a hallmark of modern earth-covered architecture.

- **Sustainability:** The Earth House Estate is designed to be highly energy-efficient, relying on natural insulation from the earth, passive solar heating, and integrated green roofs.

2. The Hobbiton Houses (New Zealand)

No list of iconic earth-covered homes would be complete without mentioning the **Hobbiton** houses in **Matamata, New Zealand**. While these homes were originally constructed as movie sets for Peter Jackson's *Lord of the Rings* films, they have become a lasting symbol of earth-sheltered architecture and inspired many real-world designs. Their distinctive style—cozy, circular doors nestled into grassy hills—evokes a sense of warmth, comfort, and a deep connection to the earth.

The **Hobbit-inspired architecture** has grown beyond film sets, with homeowners across the world building similar homes that mimic the charming, fairytale-like qualities of Hobbiton. In New Zealand, some of these homes have even been repurposed into fully functional residences or tourist accommodations, drawing visitors from all over the world who want to experience life in a home that feels as though it's part of the landscape.

- **Cultural Influence:** The Hobbiton homes reflect the cultural love of the natural world in New Zealand, where the landscape plays a central role in both everyday life and the national identity. The homes are a playful yet powerful reminder that architecture can be whimsical while still being deeply connected to nature.

- **Architectural Significance:** While initially designed for film, Hobbiton has become an enduring example of how **earth-covered homes** can evoke feelings of comfort and sustainability. It has also inspired architects and home-owners to embrace more organic, playful designs in their earth-covered projects.

3. The Malator House (Wales, United Kingdom)

The **Malator House**, often referred to as the "Teletubby House," is an iconic earth-covered home located in Pembrokeshire, Wales. Designed by the architectural firm **Future Systems** for a British politician, the house is known for its minimalist, modern design, with a grass-covered roof and a **glass façade** that offers sweeping views of the coast.

Malator's design is striking in its simplicity—its structure is essentially hidden beneath the earth, with only a glass wall and a single doorway revealing its presence. The home's low profile and **camouflage design** minimize its impact on the landscape, making it appear as though it's a natural part of the coastal environment.

- **Design Influence:** Malator's sleek, minimalist design

demonstrates how modern architecture can integrate with the natural environment without compromising on aesthetics or sustainability. Its focus on **energy efficiency** and passive solar heating also sets a standard for eco-friendly homes.

- **Sustainability:** With its green roof, natural insulation from the earth, and strategic use of glass for natural light, Malator is an excellent example of how earth-covered homes can reduce energy consumption while maintaining a modern, luxurious feel.

4. The Villa Vals (Switzerland)

Tucked into the mountainside near the famous **Therme Vals** spa in Switzerland, the **Villa Vals** is a stunning example of an earth-covered home that combines luxury with sustainability. Designed by **SeARCH and CMA Architects**, the home is built into a steep slope, with a circular opening in the façade that provides expansive views of the Swiss Alps.

The design of Villa Vals allows it to disappear into the landscape, preserving the natural beauty of the area. Its position within the mountain provides natural insulation, reducing the home's reliance on artificial heating in the cold Alpine climate. The home's interior is a modern, open-concept space that balances comfort with energy efficiency.

- **Cultural Influence:** The Villa Vals reflects Switzerland's emphasis on **environmental conservation** and the country's architectural tradition of blending buildings into the mountainous landscape.

- **Award-Winning Design:** Villa Vals has received numerous awards for its innovative approach to integrating architecture with the landscape, making it one of the most celebrated examples of modern earth-covered homes.

5. The Desert House (Arizona, USA)

In the heart of the Arizona desert lies **The Desert House**, an innovative earth-covered home designed to withstand the extreme heat of the desert while blending into the arid landscape. This home uses the earth's natural insulating properties to keep the interior cool during scorching summers and warm during cool desert nights.

The **underground design** protects the home from the harsh desert sun, while the use of natural materials, such as stone and adobe, enhances its connection to the environment. The Desert House also features a **rainwater harvesting system** and **solar panels**, making it almost entirely self-sufficient.

- **Regional Influence:** The design of The Desert House is heavily influenced by traditional Southwestern and Native American architectural practices, which have long relied on the earth for insulation and protection from the elements.
- **Sustainability:** The Desert House showcases how earth-covered homes can thrive in extreme climates, providing a comfortable, energy-efficient living space that also conserves water and resources.

How Cultural Influences Shape Earth-Covered Homes

While earth-covered homes share a common goal of sustainability and environmental integration, they also reflect the unique cultural and environmental influences of the regions in which they are built.

- **Scandinavian Earth Homes**: In countries like Sweden and Norway, earth-covered homes often incorporate minimalist designs with large windows to maximize natural light during the long winter months. These homes are typically designed to be highly energy-efficient, with features like **triple-glazed windows**, **green roofs**, and **geothermal heating systems**.
- **Mediterranean Earth Homes**: In contrast, earth-covered homes in Mediterranean regions, such as Greece or southern Italy, often incorporate **courtyards**, **terracotta tiles**, and **stone walls** to reflect the local architectural style. These homes are designed to stay cool in the summer, using the earth's natural insulation to protect against the intense heat.

The interplay of culture, climate, and tradition creates a rich diversity of earth-covered homes around the world, each uniquely suited to its environment.

Award-Winning Sustainable Designs

As sustainable building practices gain recognition, many earth-covered homes have earned awards for their innovative designs and environmental impact. Architects who design these homes are leading the way in the **green building movement**, proving that sustainability and beauty can go hand in hand.

- **The Vals Earth House** in Switzerland, for example, has won several architectural awards for its seamless integration into the Alpine landscape and its energy-efficient design.
- **The Desert House** in Arizona has been praised for its ability to provide sustainable, off-grid living in one of the harshest climates on earth.

These award-winning homes demonstrate that earth-covered architecture is not just a niche design trend, but a **viable solution** for sustainable, comfortable living in a wide range of environments.

Conclusion: From the rolling hills of New Zealand's Hobbiton to the minimalist elegance of Switzerland's Villa Vals, earth-covered homes around the world are redefining modern living. These homes represent more than just innovative architecture—they embody a philosophy that living spaces should be **in harmony with nature**, not in opposition to it. By drawing on cultural influences, responding to environmental challenges, and embracing sustainability, earth-covered homes offer a glimpse into the future of architecture.

Now that we've seen the possibilities, it's time to take the next step: How do you make your own earth-covered dream home a reality? Let's explore the practicalities of planning and building your sustainable future.

Eco-Villages and Sustainable Communities

Across the globe, people are rethinking how we live—not just as individuals, but as communities. **Eco-villages** and **sustainable communities** have emerged as models for living in harmony with nature, where shared resources, communal goals, and sustainable practices create an environment that is both **socially connected** and **environmentally responsible**. Many of these communities are centered around **earth-covered homes**, offering residents a unique way to live lightly on the earth while enjoying the benefits of a supportive, like-minded group of neighbors.

In this chapter, we'll explore some of the world's most inspiring eco-villages and sustainable communities, examining how they are designed, the benefits they offer, and how communal living works in harmony with individual privacy. We'll also take a glimpse into the daily life of an eco-village resident living in an earth-covered home, offering insight into what it's like to be part of a community that places sustainability at its core.

Examples of Communities Built Around Earth-Covered Homes

Across the world, eco-villages and sustainable communities have become proving grounds for innovative living, where **earth-covered homes** and eco-friendly practices are not just individual choices but community standards. These villages demonstrate the power of collective living when sustainability is a shared value.

1. Findhorn Ecovillage (Scotland)

One of the most well-known eco-villages is **Findhorn**, located on the northeastern coast of Scotland. Founded in the 1960s as a spiritual and ecological community, Findhorn has since evolved into a thriving **sustainable village**. It serves as a global example of what's possible when people come together with a commitment to **living in harmony with the environment**.

At Findhorn, **earth-covered homes** are a central feature of the village's architectural landscape. Built with sustainability in mind, these homes take advantage of natural insulation, passive solar design, and **local materials**, such as clay and wood. The homes blend seamlessly into the landscape, with green roofs and berms that reduce energy use and make the structures nearly invisible in the rolling Scottish countryside.

- **Community Benefits**: Residents share resources such as **community gardens**, **renewable energy systems**, and **communal spaces** for gatherings and events. By living in close connection with nature and each other, the people of Findhorn demonstrate how eco-friendly living can also foster deep **social bonds** and a strong sense of community.

- **Sustainability Features**: The eco-village has a **wind farm**, **rainwater harvesting systems**, and **permaculture gardens** that supply much of the community's food. Earth-covered homes are designed to minimize heat loss during Scotland's cold winters, reducing the need for external heating.

2. BedZED (Beddington Zero Energy Development, UK)

Located in the United Kingdom, **BedZED** is a pioneering example of a **zero-energy** sustainable housing community. While not all of the homes in BedZED are earth-covered, the community's commitment to low-impact living makes it a model for future urban developments. BedZED was built with the goal of achieving **carbon neutrality**, and it incorporates numerous eco-friendly technologies, including **solar panels**, **rainwater recycling**, and **sustainable materials**.

Although BedZED's homes are not fully underground, they make use of earth-covered **berms** and **green roofs** to improve insulation and reduce energy use. The development's focus on **energy efficiency**, **water conservation**, and **renewable energy** makes it a powerful example of how sustainable communities can thrive in urban and suburban environments.

- **Community Benefits**: Like Findhorn, BedZED fosters a strong sense of community through shared resources and communal spaces. Residents share **electric vehicles**, participate in **carpooling**, and make use of **shared gardens** to reduce their environmental impact.

- **Sustainability Features**: Every home at BedZED is designed to be energy-efficient, with **high insulation, triple-glazed windows**, and **rainwater harvesting systems**. Solar panels provide much of the energy needed for the community, and the homes are designed to maximize **natural ventilation** and **daylight**.

Benefits of Living in an Eco-Village

Living in an eco-village or sustainable community offers a number of unique benefits that go beyond simply living in an energy-efficient home. The focus on **community-driven sustainability** and **shared resources** creates an environment that is not only good for the planet but also fosters **personal well-being** and a strong sense of **belonging**.

1. Shared Resources

One of the primary benefits of living in an eco-village is the opportunity to share resources, which can significantly reduce the community's environmental footprint. Whether it's shared **transportation**, **energy systems**, or **food production**, eco-villages maximize efficiency by pooling resources that would otherwise be duplicated in traditional individual homes.

- **Renewable Energy Systems**: Many eco-villages, such as Findhorn, generate power through **shared wind turbines** or **solar farms**, ensuring that the community has access to clean energy without the need for each household to install its own system.
- **Shared Gardens and Farms**: Community gardens are a hallmark of eco-villages, where residents grow their own food together using **organic** and **permaculture** methods. This not only reduces the environmental impact of food production but also fosters a sense of collaboration and connection to the land.

2. Community-Driven Sustainability

In an eco-village, sustainability is not just an individual effort—it's a collective goal that is woven into the fabric of everyday life. The communal mindset means that everyone contributes to reducing waste, conserving water, and minimizing energy use.

- **Collective Decision-Making**: Many eco-villages operate on a **consensus model**, where residents make decisions about the community's sustainability practices together. This ensures that everyone's voice is heard and that the village's goals align with the values of its residents.

- **Reduced Consumption**: By sharing resources and embracing **minimalist living**, eco-village residents often consume less than those living in traditional communities. This can lead to both **environmental** and **financial** benefits, as households spend less on energy, water, and goods.

3. Social Connection and Support

One of the most significant benefits of living in an eco-village is the sense of **social connection** it provides. Unlike traditional suburban or urban neighborhoods, where neighbors may rarely interact, eco-villages are designed to foster **community engagement** and **mutual support**.

- **Shared Spaces**: Many eco-villages feature **communal spaces**, such as dining halls, recreational areas, and gardens, where residents can gather for meals, social events, or work together on projects. This creates a strong sense of community and reduces the isolation that can come with modern living.
- **Mutual Support**: In an eco-village, residents often support each other through **shared child-rearing**, **elder care**, or **communal work** projects. This creates a sense of interdependence and strengthens the bonds between neighbors.

Designing Homes for Communal Living While Respecting Privacy

While eco-villages emphasize community, they also respect the need for **privacy** and **individual space**. Earth-covered homes in these communities are designed to strike a balance between shared living and personal autonomy, allowing residents to enjoy the benefits of communal life without sacrificing their independence.

1. Home Design for Privacy

Earth-covered homes in eco-villages often use natural landscaping and **strategic positioning** to create private spaces for residents. For example, homes may be built into **hillsides** or surrounded by **berms**, providing natural barriers that offer privacy without the need for fences or walls.

- **Private Courtyards**: Many earth-covered homes in eco-villages feature **private courtyards** or **garden spaces** that allow residents to enjoy the outdoors in solitude. These spaces are often designed with natural materials, blending seamlessly into the landscape while providing a retreat from the communal areas.
- **Soundproofing**: The natural insulation of earth-covered homes provides excellent **soundproofing**, ensuring that residents can enjoy peace and quiet within their own homes, even in a densely populated eco-village.

2. Communal Spaces and Shared Living Areas

While privacy is important, eco-villages also emphasize the value of **communal spaces** where residents can come together. These spaces are often designed to be multifunctional, serving as places for **social gatherings**, **shared meals**, or **community meetings**.

- **Shared Kitchens and Dining Halls**: Some eco-villages, such as **The Farm** in Tennessee, have shared kitchens or dining halls where residents take turns cooking meals for the community. This not only reduces food waste but also strengthens the sense of camaraderie and shared purpose.
- **Common Workspaces**: Eco-villages often feature shared workspaces for **crafts**, **gardening**, or **community projects**, allowing residents to collaborate on sustainability initiatives.

Story: An Eco-Village Resident's Daily Life in an Earth-Covered Home

Clara, a resident of an eco-village in northern Spain, lives in a beautifully designed **earth-covered home** that is nestled into the hillside, overlooking the community's sprawling permaculture gardens. Clara and her neighbors share a commitment to **sustainable living**, and their homes are designed to have minimal impact on the environment while providing maximum comfort.

Each morning, Clara wakes up to the sound of birds singing, her home naturally insulated by the earth around it. Despite the home being partially underground, the large **south-facing windows** bring in plenty of natural light, making the space feel bright and airy. After breakfast, she steps outside to help tend the **community garden**, where residents work together to grow vegetables, herbs, and fruit.

The eco-village operates on a **time-banking system**, where residents contribute to the community in exchange for goods and services. Today, Clara spends her morning harvesting vegetables, which she later brings to the shared kitchen for a **communal lunch**. The afternoon is spent in one of the community's **workshops**, where residents discuss new ideas for improving water conservation and expanding their solar energy system.

After a productive day, Clara returns to the quiet of her earth-covered home, where the thick earthen walls provide peace and solitude. While she values the sense of community, she also appreciates the privacy her home offers—a perfect balance between communal living and personal space.

Conclusion: Living in an eco-village built around earth-covered homes offers a unique way to experience sustainability, community, and privacy. These communities demonstrate that it's possible to live in harmony with both nature and each other, creating a lifestyle that is fulfilling, connected, and deeply respectful of the environment.

Now that we've explored the benefits of eco-villages and sustainable communities, let's look at the **practical steps** you can take to build your own earth-covered home, from finding the right land to working with eco-friendly architects and builders...I can recommend one for sure ;)

The Future of Earth-Covered Homes

As the world becomes more conscious of its environmental impact, earth-covered homes are not just a sustainable solution for today—they represent the future of architecture. The next generation of **earth-sheltered homes** pushes the boundaries of design, technology, and urban planning, offering even more **eco-friendly**, **energy-efficient**, and **smart** living spaces. From cutting-edge designs to visionary projects, the future of earth-covered homes is evolving to meet the demands of a rapidly changing world.

In this chapter, we'll explore the latest innovations in **earth-covered architecture**, the integration of **renewable energy** and **smart technology**, and the exciting potential for these homes to shape **urban living**. We'll also look at a case study of a futuristic earth-covered community currently in development, offering a glimpse into the bold possibilities that lie ahead.

*Cutting-Edge Designs and the Next Generation of
Earth-Sheltered Architecture*

Earth-covered homes have always been about blending architecture with nature, but the next generation of these homes takes this idea to new heights. Architects and designers are pushing the envelope with **sleek, modern designs** that combine aesthetic appeal with environmental sustainability. These homes are no longer seen as niche or alternative; they're becoming **architectural marvels** that challenge traditional ideas about what a home can be.

1. Organic Architecture Meets Technology

One of the most exciting trends in earth-covered homes is the fusion of **organic architecture** with cutting-edge technology. Designers are creating homes that look like they've grown out of the landscape, with **curved, fluid shapes** and **natural materials** that blend seamlessly with the environment. These homes often use advanced construction techniques, like **3D printing** with eco-friendly materials, to create unique, futuristic forms that wouldn't be possible with traditional building methods.

For example, architects are experimenting with **biophilic design principles**, which focus on creating spaces that enhance the connection between humans and nature. This includes incorporating natural elements like **living walls, water features**, and **native plants** into the structure itself, creating homes that are not only energy-efficient but also restorative and calming to live in.

2. Underground Skyscrapers

As cities grapple with limited space and growing populations, some architects are turning the idea of a skyscraper on its head—literally. The concept of **underground skyscrapers**, sometimes referred to as "earthscrapers," involves building down into the earth rather than up into the sky. These massive underground structures are designed to house thousands of people while using the surrounding earth for **natural insulation** and **energy efficiency**.

Earthscrapers are still in the conceptual phase, but they represent a bold vision for the future of high-density living. These structures could help solve the problem of urban sprawl by providing **vertical housing** that doesn't consume above-ground space. They could also be designed with **renewable energy systems**, **green spaces**, and **water recycling** systems to create self-sustaining communities beneath the earth.

Integration of Renewable Energy and Smart Technology

While earth-covered homes already excel at energy efficiency, the future of these homes will likely see even greater integration of **renewable energy** and **smart technology**. This will make them not only more sustainable but also more connected and adaptable to the needs of their inhabitants.

1. Renewable Energy Integration

Many earth-covered homes already benefit from **passive solar heating**, **natural insulation**, and reduced energy use, but the next step is to make them **completely energy-independent**. By integrating **solar panels**, **wind turbines**, and **geothermal heating and cooling** systems, future earth-covered homes could generate all the energy they need, making them **net-zero energy** homes.

For example, homes could be designed with **solar shingles** embedded directly into the roof, or even **biophotovoltaic systems**, which generate energy through photosynthesis. Combined with **battery storage systems**, these homes would not only meet their own energy needs but could also feed excess energy back into the grid, contributing to a more sustainable energy system on a larger scale.

2. Smart Home Technology

Smart home technology is already becoming a staple in modern living, but for earth-covered homes, this technology can take sustainability to the next level. By using **smart thermostats**, **energy-efficient appliances**, and **automated systems** that monitor and adjust energy use, future earth-covered homes will be more efficient and responsive than ever before.

Imagine a home that can **automatically adjust its temperature** based on weather conditions, **open and close windows** for optimal airflow, or **harvest rainwater** when sensors detect a storm. These homes could even use **artificial intelligence (AI)** to predict energy use and adjust systems accordingly, reducing waste and ensuring that the home operates at peak efficiency.

Urban Applications for High-Density Populations

As cities grow and space becomes more limited, **earth-covered homes** offer a solution for **high-density urban living** that doesn't sacrifice sustainability or green space. Urban planners are beginning to explore how these homes can fit into city environments, from small developments to large-scale communities.

1. Earth-Covered Homes in Urban Green Spaces

One of the most promising applications of earth-covered homes in cities is their ability to be built into **urban green spaces**. By integrating homes into **parks**, **hillsides**, or even beneath existing infrastructure, cities can increase housing density while preserving much-needed green areas. These homes would have minimal visual impact, maintaining the aesthetic appeal of the landscape while providing energy-efficient housing solutions.

In cities where land is at a premium, earth-covered homes can also be built into **abandoned or underused spaces**. For example, disused quarries, former industrial sites, or even vacant lots could be repurposed as sustainable, earth-sheltered housing developments, offering affordable and eco-friendly homes in areas that might otherwise go to waste.

2. Eco-Districts: Earth-Covered Homes as Part of Sustainable Urban Communities

Some forward-thinking cities are exploring the concept of **eco-districts**, where entire neighborhoods are designed with sustainability as the primary focus. In these districts, earth-covered homes could play a central role, offering residents energy-efficient housing that blends seamlessly with green spaces, renewable energy systems, and sustainable transportation options like **bike-sharing** or **electric car charging stations**.

By designing these communities to be **self-sufficient**, with **shared resources** like solar power grids, community gardens, and water recycling systems, eco-districts could become the blueprint for **sustainable urban living**. Earth-covered homes would contribute to this vision by offering **low-impact housing** that supports the district's overall sustainability goals.

Visionary Projects That Push the Boundaries of Sustainability

Across the globe, visionary architects and developers are working on projects that push the boundaries of what's possible in sustainable architecture. These projects combine cutting-edge technology with forward-thinking design to create homes and communities that go beyond current standards of sustainability.

1. The ZEB Pilot House (Norway)

The **ZEB Pilot House**, designed by **Snøhetta** in Norway, is a groundbreaking example of a **zero-emission building** that integrates **earth-sheltering principles** with the latest in renewable energy technology. The home is designed to produce more energy than it consumes over its lifetime, thanks to a combination of **solar panels, geothermal energy**, and **passive solar heating**. Its design also incorporates **natural insulation** from the earth, reducing the need for artificial heating and cooling.

The ZEB Pilot House is not just an individual home—it serves as a **living laboratory** for sustainable architecture, with researchers studying its performance over time to develop new technologies and methods for achieving zero-emission buildings.

2. Desert Future Village (United Arab Emirates)

In the harsh climate of the **United Arab Emirates**, architects are developing the **Desert Future Village**, a visionary community built entirely of **earth-covered homes**. Designed to withstand the extreme heat and arid conditions of the desert, the homes are built into the ground, using the earth as a natural insulator to keep the interiors cool.

The village will be powered entirely by **renewable energy**, with a focus on **solar power** and **desalination technology** to provide clean water. The goal is to create a community that is **self-sustaining**, even in one of the world's most extreme environments, and to serve as a model for future developments in other desert regions.

Case Study: A Futuristic Earth-Covered Community in Development

One of the most exciting earth-covered communities currently in development is the **Gaia Project** in the Netherlands. This **self-sustaining eco-village** is being designed as a prototype for future urban living, combining **earth-covered homes**, **renewable energy systems**, and **smart technology** to create a zero-emission community.

The Gaia Project will feature **50 earth-covered homes** that blend into the landscape, with green roofs and **natural insulation** from the surrounding earth. Each home will be equipped with **solar panels**, **rainwater harvesting systems**, and **AI-powered energy management systems** that optimize the use of renewable energy throughout the community.

The community will also include **shared gardens**, **community workspaces**, and **recreational areas**, promoting social connection while minimizing the environmental footprint of its residents. The Gaia Project is set to break ground in the next few years, and its developers hope it will serve as a model for sustainable urban living in the 21st century.

Conclusion: A Call to Action

As we've seen throughout this book, earth-covered homes offer a sustainable, comfortable, and innovative way to live in harmony with the environment. The future of these homes is bright, with cutting-edge designs, renewable energy integration, and smart technology pushing the boundaries of what's possible. Whether you're considering building your own earth-covered home or simply exploring sustainable living options, the time to take action is now. Embrace the opportunity to be part of this movement and help create a more sustainable future for generations to come.

12

Closing thoughts from John Wilder

Embracing the Future of Sustainable Living

As an architect and self-builder, I've spent years exploring innovative ways to build homes that not only meet our needs but also honor the environment. Earth-covered homes—these hidden gems beneath the landscape—have proven to be one of the most compelling solutions I've encountered. They offer sustainability, energy efficiency, aesthetic appeal, and cost savings all wrapped into one beautifully harmonious living experience.

Sustainability has always been the guiding principle of earth-covered homes. These homes are designed to work with nature, not against it. By using the natural insulation provided by the earth, we reduce energy consumption, lower carbon footprints, and help conserve resources for future generations. When you live in an earth-covered home, you're not just reducing your impact on the planet—you're embracing a way of life that leaves the world in better shape for those who come after us.

Energy efficiency is another standout feature. Earth-covered homes are naturally cool in the summer and warm in the winter. The surrounding earth acts as a thermal buffer, stabilizing indoor temperatures and drastically reducing the need for heating and cooling systems. I've seen firsthand how these homes cut energy bills by as much as 80%. And with the integration of renewable energy sources like solar panels, wind turbines, or geothermal systems, you can achieve true self-sufficiency.

Then there's the **aesthetic appeal** of earth-covered homes. These structures offer more than just a place to live—they're a seamless part of the landscape. Whether nestled into a hillside or covered with a green roof, they blend naturally with their surroundings, making them ideal for anyone who values harmony between their home and the environment. Unlike traditional homes, which often dominate the landscape, earth-covered homes feel like they belong to the earth, not just placed on it.

And of course, we can't ignore the long-term **cost savings**. While the initial investment in building an earth-covered home may be higher due to specialized construction techniques and materials, the savings over time are remarkable. From lower energy bills to reduced maintenance costs, these homes quickly pay for themselves. The resilience they offer—protection from weather, fire resistance, and minimal wear and tear—means fewer repairs and a longer lifespan for your investment.

Taking the First Step Toward Sustainable Living

If you've been inspired by what you've read, I encourage you to take that first step toward building your own earth-covered home or learning more about the possibilities. It doesn't have to happen overnight, but every great project begins with research and a vision. Whether you start by looking into the practicalities of construction, consulting with an architect who specializes in sustainable designs, or simply dreaming about what your future home might look like, the most important thing is to get started.

Perhaps you're not ready to build just yet, but even educating yourself further on the subject is progress. Attend workshops, visit eco-villages, or tour existing earth-covered homes to see them in action. Once you begin to see what's possible, it's hard not to imagine yourself living in a home that offers both comfort and environmental stewardship.

The Future of Sustainable Living Is Not Above the Earth, but Within It

As we look to the future, the demand for **sustainable living** will only continue to grow. Earth-covered homes are not just a trend or a niche; they are a solution that addresses the most pressing issues of our time—climate change, energy consumption, and our relationship with the planet.

If there's one message I hope you take away from this journey, it's this: The future of sustainable living is not above the earth, but **within** it. Building an earth-covered home isn't just about creating a shelter. It's about adopting a lifestyle that reflects your commitment to sustainability, innovation, and a **better way of living**—for yourself, your family, and the planet.

So, whether you're ready to build today or still gathering ideas for tomorrow, I urge you to take the first step. The future is here, waiting for you beneath the surface, in homes that are as beautiful and resilient as the earth itself. And the best part? It's a future that you can help shape, one home at a time.

If you've enjoyed this guide it would mean the world to me if you'd take a moment to leave a review. It makes all the difference to others stumbling upon my tuppence worth and maybe making a small change that helps make a big change for us all

If you're keen to learn a little more please check out my other

titles including off grid living and shipping container homes.

Thank you

John

www.ingramcontent.com/pod-product-compliance
Lightning Source LLC
Chambersburg PA
CBHW071306140726
47996CB00005B/1656